CW00982943

ACADEMIC UNDRESS

An account of and guide to the
conduct of life classes
and
attitudes to nudity in public

by
Thomas Alexander
an alias/nom de plume/nom de pose
of many including
Emeritus Professor Tom Preston MA Cantab.
Fellow of the Royal Society of Arts

Published by

MELROSE BOOKS

An Imprint of Melrose Press Limited
St Thomas Place, Ely
Cambridgeshire
CB7 4GG, UK
www.melrosebooks.com

FIRST EDITION

Copyright © Tom Preston 2006

The Author asserts his moral right to
be identified as the author of this work

Cover designed by Bryan Carpenter

ISBN 1 905226 38 1

All rights reserved. No part of this publication may be reproduced,
stored in a retrieval system, or transmitted, in any form or by any means
electronic, mechanical , photocopying, recording or otherwise,
without the prior permission of the publishers.

This book is sold subject to the condition that it shall not,
by way of trade or otherwise, be lent, re-sold, hired out or
otherwise circulated without the publisher's prior consent
in any form of binding or cover other than that in which
it is published and without a similar condition including this
condition being imposed on the subsequent purchaser.

Printed and bound in Great Britain by:
CPI Bath, Lower Bristol Road,
Bath, BA2 3BL, UK

DEDICATION

To all those from whose shoulders
the mantle of Prynne* has fallen.
Amateurs/volunteers/professionals
and artists/artists' models

* Prynne was the first known model of Grecian fame (see p. xxx)

ACKNOWLEDGEMENTS

Foremost on the list of those without whose encouragement this tome would still be embryonic are Emily G Bullock, her mother Sarah Moore of Poole whose editorial and word-processing skills were quintessential as amanuensis as co-editors: also, Joyce Pawley of France. In chronological sequence those who have contributed to the author's understanding of the subject are: Pamela Boyd of Alberta; the studios of Doris and Denis O'Connor in Edmonton and all in their Thursday evening group; Georges DesRosiers, Elizabeth and others; Prof Harry Wolfarth. Those whose drawings were kindly given with permission to publish include Len Gittens; VanEyck and her clients in London; the Van Gogh museum in Amsterdam and their Sunday morning open studio; the Johnannesburg multi-racial group; studios in Hyderabad, India; the studios in Winchester University, Camden Town, Exeter St Luke's College, Paignton Adult Education and the Heatherley; San Carlos in Mexico city; RAM in London; Academie la Grande Chaumier in Montparnasse, Paris, and many more.

Professors Bryan Neale RA and Carol Weight at the RCA; Bournemouth and Poole College of Art - especially Said Dai, Francis Hatch and Eddy Foulstone, Christine and Susan; and John Bowen in Poole. Sue Wilkes, Kate Vaughan, Christine in the Dordogne; Avril Darby and her Monday group in Bournemouth; Christie, Sara Videan and John Meaker, at Sherbourne House; Meriel Hoare; others in Dorset, especially Andrew Hope; Rosemary Welsh and her mother; Bridget Woods of West Dean.

EXPLANATION OF OUR TITLE

Academic dress is the well-known cap, hood & gown regalia associated with universities and learned office.

The euphemism used for life models in art schools was: Academic poses = gracefully and elegantly arranged nudes.

So *academic undress* implies nude modelling for artistic purposes, being the opposite of academic dress.

The illustrations herein come from modern studios, to contrast with those of a couple of centuries ago, so as to illuminate both the changes of attitude and architecture. Not only have the light and heating changed but also some, but not all, of the attitudes towards those who are prepared to 'get their kit off'.

The target readership is all students of life, both amateur and professional artists, tutors, administrators and MODELS, experienced or novice. The authors are especially critical of some architects whose purpose built studios for life classes leave much to be desired and reveal little understanding of the focus of such - the **MODEL**

There is a need in many studios for many more people from all walks of life, ALL ages, ALL physiques, BOTH Sexes, ALL races and colours, tall, short, fat, thin, muscular, dark, blond, bald, to sit as nude models.

There is freedom to be found in taking the plunge and sitting silently and motionless in a sort of Yoga stillness. There is nothing to fear but fear, yet many feel horror at the thought of being themselves.

Academic Undress

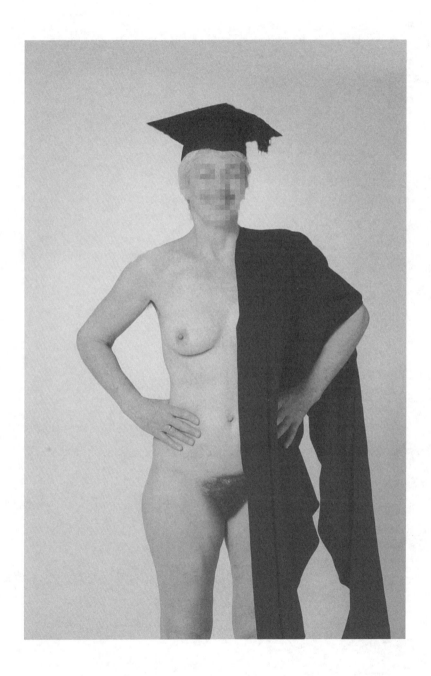

WARNING

CAVEAT

There is some evidence, from those who have taken up modelling late in life, that it can become addictive. It may be that the mental preparation for the physical effort of needing to remain still and without emotion releases some adrenaline or other pleasurable hormones.

Certainly, some models do find that their egos need to be massaged by occasional requests for them to pose. Some even become jealous of rivals who may be booked more frequently.

There is also the Biophilia component. This is literally "love of life" and is generally applied to those who enjoy recreation in their gardens and communing with nature, the sense of well-being that suffuses those who have shed the stress of urban existence. It is even a component of the release from the constraints of civilised life, which the naturists claim. Most of the genuine who have discovered the secret wonder of nudity do not talk about it for fear of being regarded as cranks.

So the second part of this caveat is to warn readers that it is all too easy to dismiss life models as eccentric cranks or worse as compulsive exhibitionists. Beware, be aware that those who bare may in fact have greater life expectancy, higher IQ and standards, than those who never experienced nature without any artifice between them, the air and the eyes of any beholders.

Postscript

It has recently become the practice of human resources staff in UK colleges of art and schools to require that all new models are cleared by the police as having no convictions for sexual crimes/

child molesting, etc, etc. This process may take many months. At interview it should be easy to detect the motives of any aspirant new model and studios usually share a list of reliable persons - for the work is never more than part-time, sporadic and ill-paid.

It should also be quite obvious to any intelligent person who has encountered 'odd types' that the body language and general mien of such persons as might pose a threat while posing is clarion. And is easily recognisable.

The present procedure does not exclude the dangerous but unconvicted.

CONTENTS

LIST OF ILLUSTRATIONS

PREFACE

The face down pose, above, is one which all models will recognise as unchallenging and not too difficult to hold. It is used here to stand for the twin contents of this booklet which:

A. Attempts to mention most topics of interest to anyone concerned with the conduct of any sort of life class.

B. Uses the life drawings taken from Flaxman's Dante of 1793, as above.

These have not been in print for two centuries - when Flaxman was among the first to teach life drawing in the Royal Academy in London. They are of interest as the engravings illuminate with great simplicity the power of the pose to communicate emotion and the strength of an accurately-placed line to convey an image to the viewer's mind from the artist's eye via the pen. They are used herein to describe the pose from a model's eyes.

The **model** is the main focus, of both this book and all studios; but some indications of the importance of the environment – heat, light – are given.

A short browse through these pages will it, is hoped, reveal that there are several intertwined topics.

A. The types of pose expected in studios from experienced models and the physiological stress they cause.

B. The etiquette of studios.

C. The essential features of studios and 'venues' where life classes can be held.

D. How to locate local studios and models - the recruitment procedures including auditions.

E. Well-known persons associated with life classes as models, organisers, commentators.

F. To create awareness of the Register of Artists' Models (RAM) www.modelreg.com

FLAXMAN

Many of the illustrations used in this booklet are derived from drawings made by the great pioneer of life drawing in the British Isles. York-born, John flourished over two centuries ago, 1756-1826. The etchings are taken from parts of his illustrations for the works of Dante published in 1807. Each has been chosen to illustrate the types of pose used in the RA life drawing studios of which Flaxman was master. See, for contrast, the sketch by Rowlandson of that studio; also the description in the 'venues' section. Many of Flaxman's compositions show the same model in the same pose from two viewpoints. For example, that re-titled 'man bites own ear' was formerly 'Impostors' and with a caption 'Beneath his savage fangs I saw him bleed'. Another example of same model in same pose from two viewpoints is the 'Mercury' pose first known as the 'Rain of Fire'. It resembles the much more recent statue, also well-known in Piccadilly Circus, London.

Those who might be interested in the numbers of models at the RA might study the excerpts and see several distinct physiques. But many were re-used in several themes.

The purpose of these illustrations is to show how some poses have so much action and balance that the model who held them for more than a few seconds must have been of superhuman talent. Experienced models, as well as novices, can discover how the model managed to stay in such poses. Other poses illustrated show crouched men carrying on their backs heavy burdens. Today Polystyrene foam can be used to simulate blocks of stone - Flaxman's students had to use imagination, see "Loads". The use of foreshortening is found in 'Malebolge'. While the 'Summit' of Malebolge has a living, human load carried as if in an angelic fireman's lift, which for two models even today would rely only on instantaneous photography. The Bridge shows some heroic poses which might be held, if the model used firmly supported parallel bars instead of the legless forks, as drawn. Other poses can be seen by the acute to have used invisible ropes or poles and hand holds disguised as spears, etc, in the final version.

The Flaxman series also illustrates an important aspect of teaching drawing, the use of outline. Ruskin was scornful of this and particularly of the use of thickness of line to draw the eye to the curvature of the form within the line. All is illusion - refinements of drawing proceed after the outline has been established.

'Schismatics' have been used to add shock-horror to the item on ghosts. The apparel and the apparition were the progenitors of the short page on Ghosts-Nu - later herein.

As long ago as 1810 when John F Flaxman was teaching in the Royal Academy in London, one prankster student was expelled for erasing the chalk marks for the models feet with a bucket of water. He remains in/unfamous but his behaviour is remembered as being beyond the pale, as is laughter behind the model's back. Flaxman taught many of the great artists yet he is not as well known, as one might expect - given the quality of his line - see the opposite page. His bust is on the left of the roof above the entrance to the Royal Academy in Burlington House, Piccadilly, London.

This pose had been included for two reasons:
1. The left leg seems on examination to be shorter than the right leg but that contributes to the illusion of the space being occupied so that the left is further from the viewers' eye than the right foot which is the closest. The left foot is also rather small by comparison with the face.
2. The age of the model is much younger than other models used by Flaxman. Older models may need more rest than younger ones! The ILO tables do NOT take this into account
The pose could be held for prolonged periods with appropriate rest breaks, especially if some prop, invisible in the sketch, supported the elbows.
For comfort, an adjustable box support for the right foot would be essential. Before rest breaks both the feet should be outlined and the position of the box on the floor. The viewer's eye level would appear to be about the same as the left calf.

This composition of several poses of the same model, of average linearity and above average muscularity and normal adiposity, illustrates the central standing pose is more tiring [even with a broom stick across the shoulders], than those with legs astride which provide greater stability – but the upstretch arms and bent spine make them just as fatiguing so with 20% time paid for rest between stints of 30 min stints: kneeling and crouching 20 min. max.

*Flaxman composed this dual pose from the same pose of one figure, probably
leaning backwards over the edge of a day-bed, or holding onto a trapeze bar.
The latter might be held for say ten minutes with a break of five – the former
for twenty with a five minute break. In either case drawn from both sides,
the reassembled with a change of verticality. It is a form of mandala, having
symmetry and rhythm. It fits the page format although cut from a much larger
group composition.*

INTRODUCTION

The intention of the authors is to encourage some changes of attitude towards life classes and their models as this burgeoning, new leisure-pursuit enters the 21st century. An objective is to encourage more people to become proud to be unprudish, part-time life models. For sadly, there still are a lot of silly ideas about nudity, relics of pseudo religious, unjoyous negative ideas.

The current shortage of good models of both sexes is such that tutors recruit over distances of up to 100 miles! Many models travel an average of 20 miles to studios. In times of under-employment this is inexcusable. One recent new recruit was offered the job at the local Labour Exchange. Others were so offended that they complained.

With earlier retirement and more time for adult education for those whose formal education often lacked any art classes, drawing can become a new interest for many; from all walks of life. For every ten, or so, students there is a need for a model prepared to sit still and unclothed without movement for three-hour periods **and many pauses for rest.**

One hesitates to suggest that modelling is a 'back to work' route for those on 'benefit'. For it is unlikely ever to be more than a part-time job, not very well paid, and calling for talents of patience and calm **rather than great pulchritude** (which means the physical beauty and classical body shape), which is often the first excuse given by the coy and reluctant for refusing any invitation to 'sit'.

Sadly, part of the reluctance to sit is that many tutors seem to regard themselves as superior in some way to the model; in this they are often deluded. For in the vicinity of a major south coast

1

resort with two art colleges and many schools and art clubs, there are some score of graduate models available, who are on call and willing , for ca £6 per hour, to sit for two hours or a full day. In other parts of the same region the going rate is £9 per hour plus travel! At £40K pa, the head of department seems unaware of this gross **fat-cat**ism. The models employed at this meagre 66% of the normal rate include a retired bank manager, several graduates of art and science, a professional musician, a ballet dancer, a post lady, a radiographer, a hotelier, a security guard, an engineer, a sports masseur, a professor and many former art students. They range in age from 18 to 80, and come in all shapes and sizes; in fact the more unusual the physique the better for teaching purposes – very tall and fat, as well as youth and beauty, are all needed so that the students encounter the full range of human form.

There is always a shortage of good models to add to the portfolio. Nothing can be worse than to have to use the same model *ad nauseam* for lack of alternatives.

The main problem is getting the right sort of person to volunteer. This often results in a class member volunteering and not infrequently happens when the 'wrong sort' of model fails to turn up on-time for a class; unpunctuality is unforgivable in life studios. When a volunteer offers the others may join in with a chorus of:

"Oh! There is no need for you to take ALL your clothes-off."

This has happened to both old and young and male and female artist models in groups where their dual role was unknown.

Thus revealing that to **undress** is in some way socially downgrading, which nudity is NOT and should never be imagined to be. The human body is the temple of the soul and all bodies are equally beautiful to informed eyes and open minds.

One basic rule of leadership is that no one should ever expect another person to do a job they are not prepared to do themselves. In the days before the world wars it was the rule in most art colleges that the young students should take it in turns to be the model. That taught them to have a proper respect for discomfort, heating and needs for rest breaks.

Some of the 'modern' art establishments who administer art classes, which the author sometimes regards as a disguised focus of under-employment, are the trendy iconoclasts of the '50s who regarded life drawing as *olde* fashioned and never modelled themselves. Those who prefer piles of bricks and pickled parts of dead livestock (commonplace in anatomical schools) to real art, can probably neither draw nor see. For the main purpose of drawing from the nude human form is to teach people to see and to look so that they can then draw any other subject accurately and convey to the viewer's mind the essence of what they saw.

It cannot be emphasised too strongly that the human mind recognises the differences between human bodies (of all subjects) far more quickly than any other subject. There are commonly recognised names for the various body parts, used in criticising an inaccurate representation. The need for nudity stems from the need for total integrity, that is continuity of lines uninterrupted by the string of a bikini, or the brightness of the whole rather than the parts which must be drawn accurately in perspective in totality. As the eye will immediately look at the distracting tiny bikini string instead of the whole body, the removal of the string solves that problem.

Another reason for terror of sitting is the strange convention of total silence in life classes , only the tutor's critical comments being audible. The models are rarely allowed to utter. WHY? Music actually improves the artistic ambience. The **total silence rule** is possibly a hangover from the days when the Lord Chamberlain only allowed nudity on stage if there was NO visible pubic hair and NO talking and NO movement. By what legal process the rules of the stage became those of the studio is not clear.

In France at the time of the Sun King and his new Academie for Painters, created to teach those who were to decorate the walls of Versailles, it became illegal for anyone to pose nude for anyone other than the new (*nu?*) Royal academicians – a closed shop. In many UK local government institutions it was, until quite recently, against the by-laws for both sexes to pose together, even if husband and wife.

Yet in Mexico where there has been an *academie* for as long as that in Burlington House, it is unusual **not** to have a man and woman together on the podium, so that students can indulge in basic comparative anatomy. In case this is misunderstood we re-phrase – it is usual to have a model of both sexes posing together simultaneously. For if one analyses the real aim of life drawing, such is essential. Yet in the English-speaking world, only very recently has it been other than rare to have several models being drawn as a group. WHY?

Some new models might find their first half-hour solo far less daunting than a solo first flight; others might not. Experienced models will admit to having progressed through stages of initial stage fright to a condition of total indifference to being the only one with 'no clothes on' in the room.

Now a few words to those who teach life classes: the majority are exemplary but a few need to be told that they urgently need some minor changes of attitude, little more than a revival of good manners and consideration. If one has been staring at another's body and subjecting it to hours of detailed scrutiny, is it not normal politeness to say "THANK YOU" at the end of the session? The Continentals often clap to show their appreciation. Instead, in some UK state-funded institutions the curt monosyllabic words from ill-educated tutors with uncouth vowels, substitute for regular enquiries about the comfort of the model, which should come from ALL teachers. Some of the inferiority-complexed, failed artists now teachers, it seems, still get a power-jolly from bullying the students and model into silent subjugation.

Another is the insensitive attitudes of some tutors. For example, one normally considerate tutor using a very fit and lovely mother of two teenagers as a specimen for an anatomy lesson, compared her body to that of a nubile double-jointed young lass who was able to show her clavicles to better advantage. Such personal comparisons are always odious, especially when the object is not expected to be other than dumb.

A rule for all studios is that the model shall always decide on when to break a pose. Only the model can know the physiological stresses. One particularly obnoxious instructress in 'fashion' has been blacklisted by the models as she imagined she was the one who decided on the medical risks of long poses! It is the number

4

one basic rule that the models take a rest break whenever they feel very stressed, having given a minute or so forewarning

A century ago the pre-Raphaelites were sued by the brother of the model who posed in the bath for Ophelia. Even in 1997 ambulances were called to treat one model who had fainted and fallen off a table. Safety at work ignored.

There is also an unwritten etiquette about disrobing, which is gradually being eroded in favour of a more logical code. Many studios fail to provide even a coat hanger and chair behind the screen they provide. The model is expected to emerge in some sort of robe or wrapper. The moment of disclosure/dis*clothes*ure is delayed until the duration of the pose is set. Models need to be quite firm about this; a pose which can be held for five minutes may be impossible to hold for fifteen. Few studios have accurate clocks visible to the model, so many provide their own egg-timer in lieu of the hour-glasses used in the old RA schools. These were turned on their side by the model and reset to be sure that a pose of one/two or four hours was exactly that, exclusive of the breaks taken by the model.

Models resuming a pose will be asked to resume it exactly and for this the floor needs to be marked with foot prints or masking tape. Very often students complain that the model has moved, when more likely they have moved or seen inaccurately. It helps models to keep the same position if there are plenty of sight-lines and mirrors to define the exact position. A sight-line is the alignment of two objects such as a window from corner with the roof-ridge of an adjacent building or a hanging item aligned with a corner of a room. Two sight-lines will fix the model's eye's position indisputably; three are even better. Any small mirror can be placed so that the model can see a limb against some background item and thus establish exactly the same pose after breaks.

It cannot be emphasised too strongly that new models need more breaks than experienced models and that serious medical problems can derive from holding a pose too long. As twisted torsos and bent limbs are far more interesting than standing to attention facing the front, a good tip is to twist as far as comfortable and then come back a few degrees to ease the muscles.

As long ago as the days of Flaxman teaching in the RA, one prankster student who erased the chalk marks for the models feet with a bucket of water was expelled and remains anonymous. Beyond the pail, as is laughter behind the model's back.

O'Keefe, the American lady painter of flowers, was so discomfited as a model that she never asked anyone to pose for her. That is an indictment of studio manners, not of life drawing as an exercise.

O'Keefe and others are included in the section on famous persons connected with life classes which is a history of some famous models with some anecdotes, for, if one's naked likeness is displayed in a public gallery, it is uplifting to know what good company one is in.

For example, Emma Lady Hamilton, Princess Pauline and her brother Napoleon were all sculpted in the nude. Famous duchesses include the Venus of Urbino, the marquis of Hertford, Balzac and Victor Hugo and Augustus Caesar, and rugger internationals were all unprudish enough to be exhibited in their birthday suits.

Those seeking anonymity have only to use a *nom de pose* or claim to be the twin double of the person in the exhibition. Models are not infrequently, greeted in the street, at a dinner or cocktail party or public transport, with "Oh! I did not recognise you with your clothes on, John" when the real name is Bill.

TRIANGULAR POSES are only possible when limbs and rump are on the same level. Some artists dislike any geometric symmetry but they are very useful for those who try to measure only in vertical and horizontal planes and ignore angles.
As a general guide, half an hour pose with ten minutes to relax limbs and regain circulation is reasonable.

7

Overheard In A Studio

Can You Knit?

Overheard by the model in a studio.

Originally attributed to Professor Tonks at the Slade pre WW1 but much embroidered.

Tonks was a medical man, a perfectionist who thought that Life studies were the key to accurate drawing. One young lady student was making little progress.

"Can you knit?" was the gruff question he posed to her after gazing in wonder at her drawing.

The answer was an enthusiastic affirmative.

"Then I suggest you leave this studio and take it up as a career."

FOREWORD

By an occasional part-time model

This is a book intended for those who wish to use some of their leisure time in the world of artistic endeavours. We all have more time to engage in non-work oriented development of aspects of our nature, which in earlier generations, only the very rich and privileged had the time, space and energy to indulge. Universities of the third age, teenagers and all ages can get together and enjoy what Addison regarded as the "proper study of mankind", that is *'Man'*, who has always been part of life classes. The hope is to encourage some changes of attitude towards the practice of life modelling as an academic experience and a leisure pursuit, as painting and drawing from the nude figure becomes more popular. Particularly to persuade more people to become unashamed of their own body and proud to be part-time life models, for sadly there still are a lot of silly prudish ideas about nudity.

One result of the current attitudes towards the nude body is a shortage of good models of both sexes. Sometimes models travel many miles to studios. This does, however, provide anonymity and reduces the risk of being recognised, by scoffers or the prudish.

With earlier retirement and people generally having more time for adult education, drawing has become a new interest for all walks of life. There is, therefore, a great demand for models prepared to pose unclothed without movement for long periods. But modelling is unlikely to be more than a poorly paid part-time job calling for patience and calm rather than great physical beauty and classical body shape (lack of which is often the first excuse given for refusing any invitation to 'sit'). In fact, the more unusual the physique the better for teaching purposes, all varieties

11

of body shapes, and not just youth and beauty, are needed so that the students encounter the full range of the human form. Artists do not want to draw only from gods and goddesses, they need all shapes and sizes. There are, in any event, no living members of any deity. In any case, it is only the very vain who think that they are beautiful. Artists need to see real people who can sit still for thirty minutes or so and after ten minutes rest resume exactly the same pose. This book is also intended to encourage more mature people to offer themselves as models. There is always a demand for genuine humanity, beings who know their own strengths and weaknesses and are willing to sit contemplating composedly whilst being drawn. Nothing can be worse than to have to use the same model ad nauseam for lack of alternatives. The artist will often 'improve' upon nature and what better way to see how others view you, than to see the improvements?

Robbie Burns, the Scottish poet, wrote of

"The Giftie gie us – to see ourselves as others see us"

That is the freebie only models get from those who are courteous enough to show their work – sadly not all.

When a volunteer offers the others may join in with a chorus of "Oh! There is no need for you to take ALL your clothes-off." reveals that it is in some way degrading to model without clothes. An alternative is suggested which is that the human body is the temple of the soul and that all bodies, no matter how old, fat, thin or weak are equally beautiful to informed eyes and open minds.

Perhaps this situation would not even arise if all art students, intent upon a teaching career, started off with the expectation that part of their training would include the experience of nude modelling themselves. In the early part of the twentieth century that was the rule in most art colleges – that the young students should take it in turns to be the model. This taught them to have a proper respect for the discomforts involved, the need for proper heating and for adequate rest breaks. Unfortunately, some of the current art establishment who administer life classes probably still regard life drawing as old fashioned, and having never modelled themselves, tend to neglect these important practical considerations. A rule for all studios is that the model should always decide on when to break a pose as only the model can know the physiological stresses.

Another reason for terror of sitting is the strange convention of total silence in life classes where only the tutor may speak and the models rarely utter. If the tutor cannot be persuaded to allow conversation the use of music may be a pleasing alternative.

Some new models might find modelling in groups far less daunting than a solo 'first flight' but others might not. Group modelling is now becoming accepted normal practice in the United Kingdom, rather later than elsewhere, although until quite recently it was against the by-laws in many districts for both sexes to pose together, even if husband and wife. It is useful to have a man and woman together on the podium so that students can see the comparative anatomies of the male and female forms.

It is important to realise that one of the main purposes of drawing from the nude human form is to teach people to see the reality of what they are viewing. Anatomy is only a minor part: the human form has the most readily recognisable curves and shapes of all possible subjects, so that the reality can be compared to the drawing and any errors identified swiftly. Once the habit of accurate observation of the human form has been acquired and mastered most can then draw almost any other subject accurately and convey to viewers' minds the essence of what was seen.

Why place such emphasis on the human form as a platform for recognising reality? I start there because the human mind recognises the differences between human body shapes far more quickly than the differences between other objects, trees for example. They can be drawn in almost any shape. With a human figure it is easy to discuss the artists' representations critically as the parts of the body have commonly-recognised names. Also, the need for nudity stems from the need for total integrity of concentration on the body as a whole without the distraction of additional lines that any form of clothing will bring. Even a bikini leaves a clarion line which is unnatural. Trunks distort proportion and hide the hip joints and much more.

The main changes of attitude required in some studios amounts to little more than awareness of good manners and consideration in the studio. Such small things as thinking about the temperature in the room, allowing adequate breaks and having the politeness to say "thank you" at the end of a session all help to attract models to come again. Continentals often clap to show their appreciation! Is that un-British or non-Anglophone?

There is also an unwritten etiquette about disrobing, which is gradually being eroded in favour of a more logical code. Many studios fail to provide even a coat hanger and chair behind some screen, they may not even provide that. The model is expected to emerge in some sort of robe or wrapper and then arrest the moment of disclosure until the duration of the pose is set. Models need to be quite firm about how long they themselves feel they can maintain a pose, as that which can be held for five minutes may be impossible to hold for fifteen. Few studios have accurate clocks visible to the model; so many provide their own egg-timer in lieu of the hour-glasses used in the old Royal Academy schools. These were set by the model and reset after a break to be sure that a pose of one, two or four hours was exactly that, exclusive of the breaks taken by the model.

Models resuming a pose will be asked to resume it exactly, and for this the floor needs to be marked with chalk outlines or masking tape. Very often students complain that the model has moved, when more likely they have moved from their original view or seen inaccurately. It helps models to keep the same position if there are plenty of sight-lines and mirrors to define their exact position. A sight-line is the alignment of two objects such as a window frame corner with the roof-ridge of an adjacent building, or a hanging item aligned with a corner of the room. Two sight-lines will fix the model's eyes positions indisputably – three are even better. A small mirror can be placed so that the model can see a limb against some background item and thus establish exactly the same pose after breaks – if the mirror is not moved.

It cannot be emphasised too strongly that new models need more breaks than experienced models and that serious medical problems can derive from holding a pose for too long. As twisted torsos and bent limbs are far more interesting than standing to attention facing the front, a good tip is to twist as far as is possible and then to come back a few degrees to ease the muscles. Start with the neck, get the eyes away from horizontal, have the head other than vertical; raise one shoulder; twist the spine; get one foot on a different plane to the other; relax. This can only be done once the weight and poise have been established. Avoid looking like a frog pinned out for dissection.

Georgina O'Keefe, the American painter of flowers, was made so uncomfortable as a model that she never asked anyone to pose for her. That is an indictment of studio manners.

OVERHEARD IN A STUDIO

Can You Knit?

Overheard by the model in a studio
This insult is reserved for female students.
"I see a greater resemblance to a glove than a hand in your sketch. I wondered if you ever knitted a glove?"
The answer was an enthusiastic affirmative.
"Then I suggest you leave this studio and take it up as a career."

WHY STUDY LIFE?
OR
WHY DO WE STUDY NUDES AS LIFE?

"Dost thou love <u>life</u>? Then do not squander time, for that's the stuff <u>life</u> is made of." (Benjamin Franklin, June 1746). An alternative version is "Then why waste time for that is the stuff <u>life</u> is made of".

The above quotation was intended to put time-wasters in their place at the turn of the seventeenth century. It was not intended to be ambiguous. Many will admit to being enchanted by life classes and meet weekly to share a studio and model. When Benjamin Franklin penned the words above, such life classes were almost unknown but they could equally apply to time spent posing, for there is much to consider when a model decides to pose in a life class as the correct use of time plays a very important part in the process. The physical strain on the model's muscles varies with each pose; some poses can be held for long periods whilst more difficult poses bring fatigue into play within a few minutes.

It has been said that drawing from life is, for artists, the same as playing the scales for musicians. All arts require a discipline for the perfection of rhythm, space and expression in balance. All include the dimension of time. Basic to the visual arts is drawing, using simple lines to create an illusion to the required scale. The shorter the pose and the more character-full the model, the easier it is to get in a few lines the essence of the subject.

One might ponder why so much emphasis is put on to learning to draw – the process by which line is used to convey some nebulous idea, later to be put into painting or sculpture. It may be an abstract notion or a very realistic representation of some person, or a portrait. The route is from the artist's eyes on to the subject, into the artist's brain and via the artist's fingers on to the paper. Thence long afterwards into the viewer's eye and brain. AND HERE IS THE TEST. If the viewer is a child then the simplistic interpretation is all that is received but if the viewer's mind is more sophisticated than the artist's, then the outcome is critically appraised.

The question so rarely posed and so often misunderstood is: "Why pose nude?" The simplistic explanation is that this gives the artists a thrill and allows them to copy the great masters' paintings in chapels, cathedrals and so on. Naked and naughty humans posing as gods and goddesses, prancing around the universe, pretending to be angels of innocence tempting the artists to rude thoughts. An even less charitable notion is that the models themselves get a kick out of it but all these ideas can be rejected if only on the grounds that so many public institutions hold life classes and exhibit and sell the 'Nude in Art'.

The actuality is that the nude human form contains an infinite variety of readily recognisable curves and planes with subtle tones. No other object is so assimilated by the human mind. Each member of the human race has hundreds of unique lines about him or her which distinguish that person from any other. That is why the whole body is used without the distraction of clothes. Furthermore, each person can arrange their limbs and muscles to display intentions and mood, in an infinite variety of ways. All this combined with the 360° vantage points possible in three dimensions suggests that the human naked body is the best possible object for pictorial representational exercises in drawing and visual art form creation.

Children first learn to recognise the image of their mother's eyes. The recognition of the shapes O X O rely upon this fact of psychology as does that of other shapes, O M O, O N O, for example. As we grow up we become more efficient at recognising the most minute differences between peoples' eyes and then their faces and bodies. Between friends we know and possible foes who we do not. The human brain is very adept at noticing the slightest variations, first in real life, and then in portraits and other representations, for example photofits.

While a camera can capture a stance realistically, the blink of a human eye is rarely enough to produce even a moderately convincing drawing. However, drawing from memory, even after such a short duration of study, can often produce an image that is more convincingly life-like than drawing from a photograph or a statue. Both these practices are deemed to be reprehensible, tantamount to a form of cheating. However, the augenblick (blink of an eyelid) or camera shutter exposure can be used effectively. Looking at a subject and blinking the eye to capture a mental image in totality is a trick for training the mind. Lord Macaulay used it and could demonstrate that after seeing a page of writing for a few minutes he could read it aloud accurately much later.

This is a James Bond espionage feat that can be used in a life class, in fact, some schools insist that for all poses the first minute should be spent 'just looking', even if the pose is only going to be held for two minutes in total. This exercise is used for training the mind to look at the entirety rather than to focus on the small detail, and it is a skill that is obtained only after considerable practice. Life classes are intent upon teaching people to overcome their natural untrained vision. The experience is unique because we are looking at another body from within our own bodies of which we have a very special concept, largely because we can only see ourselves by using a mirror. Our minds distort our own image of ourselves and we are rarely capable of an honest self-portrait. It is a strange fact that beginners in life classes usually tend to impose their own body physique on the model they are currently drawing, distorting towards some sub-conscious notion of reality. Very thin people and very fat people with an average model do not believe their own eyes. The average become thin or fat; but when they look at their own opposites, the mental incredulity becomes even more evident. The author did experiments with engineering students, architects and others to prove the need for designers to become aware of the realities of the human form rather than infantile perceptions.

It also helps when trying to convert a three-dimensional reality into a two-dimensional likeness to understand how we see stereoscopically. Our binocular vision is basically two 'cameras' (eyes) whose output is merged into one image in the back of the brain. In infancy we learn to touch things to establish where they are in relation to ourselves by inverting the images and gauging distance and angles. The visual image of what is outside our bodies is in fact an illusion. It exists only in the nerves inside our cranium. This is confirmed by the fact that in the dark we can visualise space and walk to avoid objects whose presence we are sure about.

If we are looking at the nude human form we deduce, without much conscious thought, major items such as sex and age from key signs. The details help us to 'read' the image. Eyes tell us which way the head is tilted, the nails demonstrate if the hand is palm up or down, or if it is the right or left. The slant of the spine is indicated by the position of the navel and the nipples when viewed from the front, and by the spinal process and buttock cleavage from the back. The major proportions which provide clues can only be seen from one viewpoint and, unless the artist is practised in 'seeing' what form the body is really taking in the current position, it is that viewpoint that novice artists assign to the drawing.

It is one thing to recognise all these. It is difficult to represent them in perspective so that all body members appear natural.

We all know that the thumb is much larger than the little finger, but a gesture can only be read by seeing the relative sizes of each finger as well as the shapes of the nails and their juxtaposition. It would be flawed to try to draw a hand as one sees it in one's clinical mind's eye, spread out with fingers splayed. Many amateurs imagine a glove bent into some gesture and try to draw that but professional artists look for shapes which when placed accurately give an illusion of the hand as it presents itself. In order to interpret the human form artistically it is also necessary to have an understanding of the bone structures and how the muscles are attached to them. Echorchée (flayed) small scale models are used with skeletons, which are sometimes actual human remains, but are more usually reproduced in plastic from casts of real bones. A ritual often pursued in life drawing classes requires a model to pose alongside a skeleton.

In another ritual, a projector is used to fit a photographic skeleton to the model's body. Surprisingly the fit is usually convincing even if a tall model is used.

Then a comparative anatomy lesson is given indicating the very precise points where the bones lie just under the skin and where muscles bulge or relax according to the load or gravity of the situation. Another exercise, which can be done in life classes to train artists to 'see', is to ask the model to move in a repeated pattern for the duration of the pose. The object is to get the students to see a particular part of the movement and to draw it bit by bit as the same aspect recurs. DuChamps' 'Nude descending the stairs' is a classic example of this technique.

The models cannot just walk up and down a flight of stairs or they will get tired very soon. Furthermore, the artist would have to wait a full cycle of all the way up and all the way down before the same movement of the pose was repeated. So, clearly there are a few tricks to learn. For a start one box can be substituted for a whole staircase, as it is the angle of perceived observation that provides the illusion of escalation. The model has to drill this moving pose beforehand so that the repetition is precise, otherwise the pose will not be successful.

This exercise encourages artists to memorise what they have seen and other techniques can also be used to aid memorisation. Some tutors install a model in an area away from the studio and the artists have to hold the pose in their minds while they return to start their work. Another variation is to hold the pose for ten minutes without drawing and then allow the model to rest whilst the students draw from memory.

The ultimate in impossible poses is the belly dance and hula hoop. Although it may be seen as an alternative to the walking pose it might provide a rhythmic mobile where the feet are always static.

Moving poses have the advantage of catching the model in 'flight' and so avoiding a pose devoid of realism. The wood etching made by Gwen Raverat in 1912 of a nude male figure in a pose akin to that of a ski-jumper in full flight is evocative of movement and of power yet was conceived long before such could be captured by cameras. The artist was a grand-daughter of

Charles Darwin, the pioneer of the notion of evolution through the process of natural selection. The pose is of course one which is impossible to hold for a second, but by repeated observation and cogitation it is possible to fix such detail as the exact angle of the pendulous appendages such as the penis, which it is unlikely the lady artist would have observed at the Slade where she studied a century ago.

In the confines of a studio the speed of flight may be such that starting or stopping may have to be achieved in too short a distance. A large clear space in the centre is needed. The model should move in a simple circle but this may cause giddiness if the circle is too small. To combat this, the model should be asked to move slowly. A central pole or a broom-stick can be used as a pivot. A larger circle can be used if a step-up on to a box, or even two steps, is introduced. The model steps up and down and moves continuously around so that the routine is repeated. The rhythm of paces can be called out and care should be taken to ensure that the same foot makes the step on to the box and that the arms swing in the same direction. A walking stick helps to maintain balance in these poses and add a point of reference for the students.

However, physical techniques alone cannot overcome artists' static responses to the 'perceived' form. It takes time, patience and repetition to free oneself of mental restraints that cramp the expression of our true personalities. This applies when we attempt to draw the nude human form, whatever media we opt to use. This practice is not easy but can be very enjoyable. In much art it is what is not stated, the silences and the blank spaces which have as much meaning as what is stated.

Life drawing, then, is about seeing how the parts of the body are arranged in space. That of course includes recognising perspective and most life poses present a very complicated perspective, rarely full frontal with limbs and spine straight. The challenge for the artist is to convey to the viewer the actual physique of the model. The exercise of drawing is to create a two-dimensional illusion of a three-dimensional reality.

OVERHEARD IN A STUDIO

Caustic remarks for Foundation class laggards – overheard by many models in many studios.

"You are holding your pencil/charcoal/brush like a knitting needle – WHY?

You were told you were neither writing words nor etching, nor knitting – when Sketching draw from the shoulder – not the hip"

ILLUSION

The aim of much drawing is to transfer to the paper some thought/emotion perception of a person so that the illusion is recreated in the mind of any informed viewer. Gombrich in his 'Art and Illusion', part IV, refers to the "expression of human passions" and the impossibility of drawing from a model who is only acting the part. He also provided examples of Egyptians able to depict 2500 years ago running and jumping, etc., which are as impossible as hoola-hooping to hold in a static pose.

It is clear that any expectation of a student to produce an illusion of such is doomed to failure. Nevertheless, action poses are possible with the aid of props and sky-hooks [ropes from beams above the podium]. In the same way, grimaces may be called for – they are possible only for short durations. Both are excellent opportunities for getting the students and those 'using' a model to copy the pose to feel how is affects them. A major failure in studios observable by models is that few stand back from their easel and look at the whole from more than half a metre. And only rarely do any other than the most experienced artists copy – mimic the pose because, so one might suppose, this might cause them to be ridiculed and embarrassed – pity.

GOMBRICH

FRESH AIR AND SUNLIGHT

The seminal text on 'Art and Illusion' was written in 1960 by Professor Sir Ernest Gombrich. While it commences with a Life Class, surprisingly no mention is made of models or Life Classes in the index, yet allusion and illusion to the human form is *partout*. Perhaps the omission reflects on the supposed inferiority of the living model to the illusion within the art-viewer's mind. It is an inescapable fact that without models there can be no Life Classes and those who have never seen a nude of the opposite sex are unlikely to appreciate the lifelike accuracy, or otherwise, of any illusion thereof they may experience in an art gallery.

The illustration before the first page is of an imaginery life-class in prehistoric Egypt school. It is a cartoon by Alaine from the 1955 New Yorker magazine, reproduced, if permission is granted, herein. The theme is an alfresco but walled life room, with the model in a pose of a typical egyptian dancer with extreme agulated arms, elbows and wrists flexed to their limits. The entire class is measuring with extended arms and stylii.

Late in Part Four, Gombrich describes an attempt in ca 1873 to get full sunlight into life classes. It is on page 273 ISBN 7148 1756 2 beside the well-known and oft-parodied *'dejeuner sur l'herbe'* by Manet painted in 1896, which doubtless provoked Horace Lecoq's ire. It had shocked the 'establishment', for sunlit nudity in public was deemed uncivilised. the scene is of a picnic on the banks of a river where two well-dressed young men chat with two undressed, nubile girls. One towelling herself after bathing, the pile of garments in the foreground tells the tale of disrobement.

The well-respected, French teacher of art, Horace Lecoq de Boisbaurand, who was critical of the indoors-only life-class routines, such as were imported to Dublin by Valencay, was allowed to experiment with models in the open air, before 1873. The illusion of a tall, bearded male model posing asleep on a bed of reeds, recreated the illusions of classical gods in myths such as were depicted by Raimondi and Durer in the 16th century. it is not known if they ever posed models outside of their studios. Rodin certainly did, chosing from a number of nude models when the weather was fine; but he also used a candle in a dark studio for other studies.

Lecoq's words were translated into English by L D Luard in 1911: "the Training of the Memory in Art and the Education of Artists".

An illusion is making the viewers' eye and brain believe something exists when it does not. We see faces in clouds.

A point to remember is that imprecision is created naturally, simply because our physical system responds in that way. The eye and brain can play tricks to create illusions we are only just beginning to understand. We do not always judge distances accurately. One simple proof of this is to draw two lines of exactly the same length, say 8cm long and 2.5cm apart, one above the other. Then put arrow-heads on the end of the top one >– < and reverse these on the lower line <– >. Be sure to make the points on the tip of all four arrows. Which now is apparently the longer?

A more recent discovery is that we are influenced by sound before sight. If we hear three percussion sounds; three gong beats, three drum beats and three bells followed by a single flash, the flash will also be remembered as a triple event. Sound has a clear-cut effect. Drawing to background music affects style; if there is a loud, staccato drumming of constant 'thumping' heavy stabbing blotches will be produced, while a more melodious Mozart violin will show the mirroring of the curves of the limbs, calf to thigh to buttock to belly to back, following a serpentine flow done with sinuous pleasure when one almost feels the harmony and proportions.

Motion can be seen in static depictions. Colours vibrate if they are strong – silver and black, orange and red. It depends on the psychology of the moment and mood exactly which seem preferable and the most vibrating. Even black and white can be made to seem to move; concentric rings of mill-stone line radii will make the blank spaces move gyrating in clockwise directions, yet they are completely blank. It is what is not there which says the most.

One reason why the early figurative models were referred to as the 'living human form' was to distinguish them from the dead. The public dissection, often of criminals, was once a popular entertainment. It is well known that two centuries ago many artists attended anatomy classes in medical schools to learn about the structure under the skin. The process of revealing from a corpse the workings of once live bodies fascinated Leonardo, Rembrandt and others.

So there are two legal ways in which the human body may be used for anatomical educational purposes; living and dead. The third, vivisection, we now discount as unlawful, especially flayling, which was popular amongst sculptors as it clarifies musculature.

CASTS

In various academies in London, during 1885, Mulready demonstrated to young students from the casts of human bodies. Asked how he taught students to improve upon nature he replied that he pointed to the imperfections on the cast model and explained how these came about. In Rome that year, the Ladies Art College instituted night classes to educate models and tried to send the idea 'back home' where there were estimated to be 500 life models living and working in London.

In 1756 the pay of the director of the life studio for the Royal Dublin Society was £110 per annum, plus extras, which paid for the hire of 'living figures', who were usually soldiers from the local barracks. The director, the retired General Charles Valencay, FRS MRIA (see Dict. Nat. Biog.) clearly had easy access to the military.

A 3D sculpture studio in which the model is central and rotates every fifteen minutes to face a new direction. The students then see their work from a new angle and rotating their work also, to correspond.

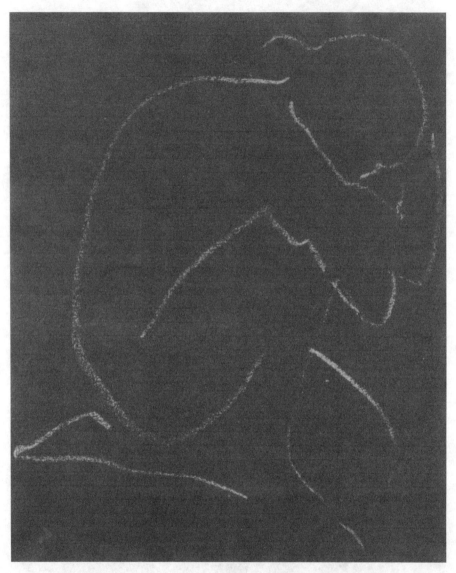

This rapid action pose was white chalk on black paper

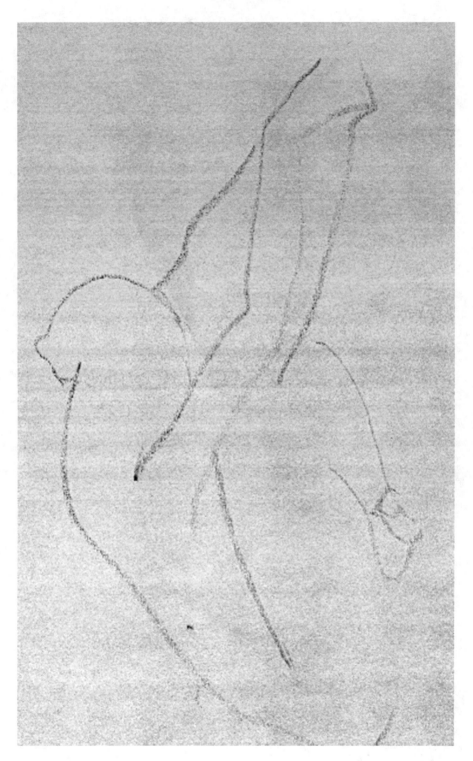

The lines are a series of short pose sketches superimposed one on another during a moving pose in which the model walked around the studio. Sometimes a leg, and later the buttocks for which the Latin polite terms is gluteus maximus , then the arms and spine attract attention and the process eye-brain to drawing hand commences. The original was charcoal on A2 paper, white, sometimes much larger sheets are used – often on the floor. One of the best-paid American painters does wall canvasses from moving poses life-sized of over 100 square feet, for which there is a waiting list: his charges are $1 million plus. A few years ago he exhibited in the Serpentine gallery.

One can just discern one pose superimposed on others in this rapid moving pose.

FAMOUS PERSONS ASSOCIATED WITH LIFE MODELS

One of the targets of this list of a few famous models is to dispel that, sadly for some, full-time bread and butter income is, and always has been, almost impossible to find. Studios need a variety of bodies of both sexes OR, if Quentin Crisp's concept of himself as a third is accepted, this should be ALL sexes; as well as all physiques, all ages, colours, hirsuteness and so on. Models for life studios are not chosen for their pulchritude. Crisp, aged 56, was, according to Victoria Gillick in the Daily Telegraph (25 November, 1999), "frankly disgusting and going to pot". He could, however, "hold a pose without twitching or moving" which is the sole essential attribute for the job.

Attitudes towards nude models throughout the ages have always been volatile. At times models have come from the highest strata of society. Three duchesses, the mistresses of various kings of France and an actress (Lily Langtree), mistress of Edward VI of England, head the list of nude models. Statues of nude Caesars exist. Often, however, nude models were relegated to the lowest social stratum. But in France there is a very strong tradition of modelling from the higher ranks of society. Agnes Sorel, mistress of Charles VII, modelled for Fouquet. Madame de Bellegarde and Madame de Noailles modelled for David's 'Sabine Women' and found no social shame in doing so. Boucher had models that included marquises. In contrast, the British attitude towards nudity was always more reserved. Robert Browning wrote a poem ridiculing a lady who wore dead birds on her hat whilst regarding nude modelling as amoral. Oscar Wilde wrote about Dorian Gray, a fictional male model.

More modern attitudes are revealed by the first career of Sir Sean Connery, described below. Here, in no particular order, are some others:

CAMPASNE

The first model for whom we have a name was Campasne, the wife of Alexander the Great, said to be portrayed in Apelles' painting of Venus alias Aphrodite (pre-400 BC). The proverb Nulla die sine linea, meaning 'never a day without drawing a line', comes from his daily routine. It is as true today as it was 24 centuries ago.

PRYNNE

Prynne was a Greek model who earned relatively high fees and gained 'largesse' from patrons, which she then squandered. Her name means sieve, and later became synonymous for all nude models, who were presumed to have the same spending habits as Prynne herself, i.e. 'easy come easy go'.

JANE
(CHRISTABEL JANE DREWRY, LATER MRS LEIGHTON-PORTER)

The death of Britain's best known newspaper artist's model, Jane, was the topic of a full page in the Daily Telegraph on 8 December 2000. She was 87 but kept this a secret, saying that she was "57 plus VAT" and still a very lively lady. She had not been tall enough to go in for fashion modelling, so instead, in her late teens became an artist's model in London. Later she won the contest for 'Venus of Kent' and subsequently, 'Britain's Perfect Girl'.

She was born Christabel Jane Drewry in 1913 in Bournemouth and married an RAF pilot and engineer, Leighton Porter, by whom she had a son born in 1953. She was a twin and an 11th child. Winston Churchill described her as Britain's secret weapon, for her adventures in the strip cartoon of the Daily Mirror were a morale booster, measurable at the front line. She was the pin-up girl of all-time fame.

Her career began in 1939 when as a model posing for a life class in Birmingham she was spotted by the cartoonist Norman Pett on a visit to his old art school. He had previously used his wife Mary as his model for the strip-cartoon which had started in 1930.

The cartoon lasted through the war with unprecedented popularity with the Forces. Cristabel became the public face of the fictional Jane, whose escapades were provocative and illustrated in poses of the unacademic 57 varieties.

By 1949 she was in the screen version of the Adventures of Jane as a film star of her own, albeit fictional life, luring secret agents in the war against evil.

Pett moved to the Sunday Despatch and a new artist, Michael Hubbard, continued the series.

SIR SEAN CONNERY

A recent item of 'news' may serve to illuminate, at least to the author's mind, some silly attitudes of many journalists and their notions of what will interest readers. It came under a headline* in the Saturday Telegraph of August 23, 2003, page 5

"ARTIST FINDS NAKED SEAN CONNERY IN HER ATTIC "

An article with photographs of sketches of a bare-chested Sir Sean (now 73) followed, with details of the artist, Mrs Hilary Buchanan, then 18 now 68, who had found her black and white drawings, as a student of the then milkman, now Scottish patriot-cum-patriarch and film star.

He was clearly suitably unsuited – but not naked; for he modestly wore a loin cloth, estimated to be five inches wide and seven long – a thong.

One Richard Demarco, who also attended the classes at the Edinburgh College of Art, declared that Sean was "a great inspiration for an artist and was amazing to paint and draw".

While Hilary, who now teaches adult education classes, recalled him as a "very solid presence… a spectacular physique". This might be attributed to his body-building and his then recent third place in the Mr Universe competition. She also recalled his "jet black hair and eyebrows", although neither are discernable from her pen and ink/charcoal drawings.

*Sadly, the headline is demonstrably untruthful.

They were drawings of a nearly naked man. There was no naked man nor was it a young knight/esquire in the flesh.

DUCHESS OF ALBA
According to a 2003 TV show on Goya, the reclining nude said
to be the Duchess of Alba is not her but a private picture painted
for a minister of the government, whose mistress was a look-
alike of the duchess. The girl in the painting is under twenty-five
whilst the duchess was aged forty at the time the picture is dated.
There are several other possible explanations: perhaps Goya was
painting from memory; he had painted the duchess clothed on
many occasions after he had become infatuated with her.

QUENTIN CRISP
Quentin Crisp, author of 'The Naked Civil Servant', is the
quintessential of the public misconception of a male model. He
was, however, as much a character actor and poseur as a poser.
Born Dennis Pratt on Christmas Day, 1909, he was the son of a
solicitor and subsequently went to a minor public school. Having
attempted and failed, to read for a diploma in journalism at Kings
College London he later became an author of several books on
such diverse topics as 'Lettering for Brush and Pen' from his work
as a draughtsman, and 'Colour in Display' from his experience as
a window dresser. He worked as a nude model in many studios.
The author has known several students who drew from him. All
praised his talent for motionless unusual poses. Others claim he
terrified young male students.

LYDIA DELECTORSKAYA
Lydia Delectorskaya was the unknown anonymous muse, secretary
and archivist of Henri Matisse. She was born in Siberia where her
father was a professorial paediatrician. She clearly adored him and
came to Paris in the hope of becoming a medical doctor. Unable
to raise the money for fees, she lived in penury in Nice, working
as a cabaret artist, casino marathon dancer and as a model.
   In 1932, she was hired by Matisse who needed a studio
assistant. She later became his model and inspired him to return
to figurative painting. Ten years later he became bed-ridden after
a colostomy. She then became his nurse and gave him a further
decade of what he regarded as his best work. It was she who fixed
his cut-outs to the pages and outlined his dancers in pink and
blue. For his cut-outs were the very essence of his art but it was she

who, under his guidance, put together his collages which were the very essence of his work. When he died in 1954 she became his archivist and organised exhibitions. Although she was given paintings worth millions which she could have sold, she donated them all to Russia.

Her biographer, Ms Hilary Spurling, who interviewed Lydia at length says that the life of Matisse was inextricably entwined with that of Lydia and they cannot be seen separately. Yet no one knows if there was any sexual relationship, a question that Hilary Spurling thinks "ought to remain unasked and unanswered". As indeed should all such studio relationships whether famed or obscure. Excess interest in the private lives of anyone – royalty, pauper, film star – is evidence of empty minds.

HORTENSE FIQUET

Paul Cezanne was thirty in 1869 when he met his nineteen-year-old wife Hortense Fiquet, a model. Their son was born in 1872 and was later to be drawn many times in the nude by his father. Cezanne, however, never drew from the nude female form; he only drew adult males for a short period in his teens when he was at the Academie Suisse. Later in life when he was inspired to draw his bathing scenes of females he returned to earlier sketches, which he had made of soldiers bathing in a river. Unsurprisingly, the forms of the women lack femininity and are anatomically rather unconvincing. The visual artistry of the paintings rests in the image as a whole, rather than their individual shapes, the amalgamation providing an illusion of beauty.

MURIEL FOSTER

In the Journal of the Pre-Raphaelite Brotherhood Studies No. 8, Fall 1999, there was a long article by Jas K Baker and C Cathy. Their tentative theory is that one of the favourite models of Waterhouse was a lady born in 1878 and who died aged 91 after a career in nursing. It is also speculated that the relationship was based on more than the fact that the artist's family included Fosters. All this is based upon a pencilled note of her name on the back of one picture and the fact that she could have been paying for her nursing training at St Thomas' Hospital by posing for Waterhouse,

*Muriel Foster – a model who was a PRB (Pre-Raphaelite favourite).
Note the relative sizes of eye and hand. Note how the hands are supported. 15
minutes with 5 minutes break.*

who later married and was rather more conventional than his Pre-Raphaelite Brotherhood 'kin'.

JERRY HALL

The Daily Telegraph of November 29, 2001 had two models in the same pose. One was a new painting of Jerry Hall reclining clad in a dark skirt and lacy blouse by Paul Benney and the other the same, of Goya's Naked Maja. It appears that the glamorous model/ actress is about to pose identically for a second time for Paul, only on this occasion in the nude. She had also, when pregnant, posed for Lucien Freud. The result was deemed by connoisseurs not to be very attractive.

DAME LAURA KNIGHT

In an apparent self-portrait, now in the National Portrait Gallery, Dame Laura chose to paint herself from a mirror while the model sits in the hair adjusting pose. The effect of the clothed version of the artist in a hat causes the viewer to ponder the choice of pose and the 'me in a hat, skirt and cardigan looking at her in the nude looking at my own back while doing up my hair, looking in a mirror from the front'. A more difficult exercise would be hard to devise. Were her hands really as shown or were they holding the hand mirror? Or were there mirrors marked with sight-lines so that she could be certain that her eyes and the pose were exactly the same for every brush stroke. In fact the identity of the model is known.

In any event the picture is without doubt the best possible example of that unique combination of a LIFE artist model. No problems with intimating the need to rest fatigued limbs and yet not disturbing a moment of concentration.

AMY LYON

The life of the girl named Amy Lyon is not as well known as her later career. She worked as a model for a quack doctor who sold beds to cure old mens' ailments. She used various semi-nude 'poses' to demonstrate and entice the rich: she even allowed clients to test the bed alongside her! These she termed ACADEMIC POSES. At a later stage in her career she changed her name to Emma Hart and married Sir Wm. Hamilton, a British Consul in Naples, after which she became famous as the companion of Lord Nelson, Lady Hamilton.

THE HON MRS (C Z) GUEST

The obituary of this American society figure, famous for her much syndicated gossip columns, appeared in the Telegraph in early November 2003. She was married to the ultra-wealthy son of the first Lord Wimbourne, of GKN and Lord Lieutenant of Ireland. Before their marriage, she modelled in Mexico for Diego Riviero. Her husband retrieved the nude art from a bar before their wedding. Her sister-in-law is known to have drawn at the Heatherley and other life studios in North America. Diego's wife Lila Kala was at one time connected with Trotsky and the communist party Marxists.

GARDNER MCKAY

Gardner McKay was described by Life magazine as the most handsome man to hit Hollywood since Cary Grant. He died aged 69 having been born in New York in 1932. His father was the advertising genius who devised for Lux soap the slogan "for that schoolgirl complexion". The family lived in Paris, Rome and Madrid, which doubtless influenced the young boy towards the arts and liberal attitudes. He also attended a dozen schools, which repeated changes would certainly have had an adverse effect on his academic development.

After two years at Cornell University he dropped-out and took up sculpting and commercial modelling in Manhattan. According to a friend from Cornell, "he sometimes stood in for the model in the life classes, and this filled the studios". It is not revealed with which gender of sculptors. After a few films he retired to his ranch in Beverley Hills where he kept a menagerie of big cats. Later he moved to Honolulu where he produced and wrote plays and an autobiography. He married in 1984 and had a son and daughter.

PRINCESS PAULINE NAPOLEON

Princess Pauline Napoleon, sister of the emperor, was born in 1780 and died 1825. She married Prince Camillo Borghese but soon tired of him and returned to Paris.

After this she posed for Canova for a nude Venus. The painting can be seen in the Borghese and is illustrated in Lord Clarke's *Feminine Beauty*. In 1810 she was expelled from the court for rudeness to the new Empress Marie Louise. Wellington bought her palace in Rue du Faubourg St Helene, which is now the British Embassy.

RODIN'S KISS
ANTONIO NARDONI AND CARMEN OR
PAULO MALATESTA & FRANCESCA RIMINI

Rodin hired for auditions up to twenty male and female models, whenever he needed inspiration from the human form. He found them in the 'model-market' in Place Pigalle, thence to a session at his studio. He used limbs and body parts from several models in some cases as is described later. For one franc per hour, twenty models of both sexes had to parade slowly around the studio until he saw an interesting pose or part; he would then tell that person to hold the pose whilst he sketched it. The poses often reflected the poor habitation/health or general [un]employment that the models had to endure. One might scratch, another pick out a splinter of wood, or another discover a flea.

'The Kiss' by Rodin is well known. The two entwined models were said by some to have been Antonio Nardoni and Carmen. Antonio was a very moral, married man who later had many grandchildren. He admitted it was a difficult pose to hold. On the other hand, the names of the models were said to have been Paulo Malatesta and Francesca da Rimini. Does it matter?

ALICE PULLEN

Also called Dorothy Dene, the names may not mean very much to many readers. Yet artistic aesthetes know her classically beautiful body from Frederick Lord Leighton's 'Bath of Psyche'. She died in obscure circumstances of peritonitis in 1886. Yet once Bernard Shaw admired her acting and beautiful speech. Despite this, she was said to have been of working class origins, from New Cross in London.

She became famous because she was the prototype of Eliza Doolittle in Pygmalion. George Bernard Shaw did not approve of Frederick Lord Leighton, whose paintings he thought were too polished and smooth, having only perfect forms. Alice was often seen near his house in Holland Park, where his studio is now open to the public. She modelled for him as the captive in Andromache and as Persephone. Although Leighton was warned, by his sisters, that there was gossip about his relationship with Alice, which he denied, he did help her to become an actress. The disapproval of that family of any infatuation with a model is further evidence of social attitudes at that time. Queen Vic only agreed to enoble an artist when she heard he had no heir.

LADY SCOTT

The widow of the polar explorer and mother of the bird artist, Lady Scott (later in her life to become lady Lady Kennet) née Kathleen Bruce died in 1947. She began her career as a sculptress in Paris where she was a student of Rodin. Whilst there, she attended 'ladies-only' life classes. According to her biographer the sight of nude male models made her physically sick. One ponders her marriages... Her son, the second Lord Kennet, was the author of a book entitled 'Eros denied' – how the child oft swings to the opposite pole of the parent!

ELIZABETH SIDDALL

Better known as 'Lizzie', model, pupil and later wife of Dante Gabriel Rosetti. She posed for several of the Pre-Raphaelite Brotherhood but as far as is known, only once, as Ophelia in a flower-strewn bath, for John Millais. There is a stained glass window in St Peter's, Bournemouth, of Liz with her distinctive profile and hair. It came from the workshops of William Morris. The Rosetti family were at great pains to sanitise her reputation as a model. They seemed to feel that being the model in a studio was somehow demeaning and inferred some lower-class origins. The family maintained that her father was a steel-master cutler in Sheffield, which is a couple of rungs up the social ladder than he was in real life – an ironmonger in Chelsea.

Her latest biography by Lucinda Hawksley (2004 Andre Deutch) recounts her discovery, aged twenty, in 1849. Her rivals were Annie Millar, Janey Morris and Fanny Cornforth – known unkindly as 'the Elephant' on account of her size. Janey was Wm Morris' wife.

EFFIE GRAY

Effie Gray, divorced wife of William Morris and later Lady Millais modelled for her husband in several paintings, none so far as is known in the nude. The 'Highlander's release', now in the Tate, is of a soldier's wife who has given herself to his guard – and is faced with a moral dilemma.

SIMONETTA

The painting of Botticelli's Venus rising from the sea is of Simonetta, the sixteen-year-old wife of Marco Vespucci, but painted from imagination after her death.

SUZANNE VALADOR

Utrillo's mother, Suzanne Valador, became a famous artist in her own right, but began as a model. She became a regular model after being spotted whilst out on her laundry delivery round and eventually modelled for Renoir. She was an intelligent woman and later offered criticism of painting techniques. Her father may also have been a painter.

HELEN & ZEUXIS

The preceding list of those models who were depicted in their totality, open in spirit (with or without garments) is, we hope, sufficient to convince readers that there is no social stigma attached to being a life model. It does not cover those whose form is only partially used. Rodin composed his sculptures from parts of many models; an arm of one, the neck of another and the foot of a third. He was not the first to recognise that perfect images of the most beautiful bodies can only be achieved by mixing the best features of several models. Cicero in his 'Rhetoric' told a story of the best Greek painter Zeuxis, who when he was asked to paint Helen, the perfection of womanhood, selected five maidens and from each compounded the image even more beautiful than any of the five.

In the 15th century, one Gerald of Flanders made a miniature of this, it is mss 10, fol 69v. in the Bibliotheek of the University of Ghent. The painter sits with his back to the viewer, with a very limited pallet of colours. He looks at a group of five pretty maidens in long robes. So the multiple pose is also as ancient as history.

Whether this may be a ruse on the part of the artist to get more than one model is an unanswerable question, either for Rodin or any others, including Zeuxis.

There are two points in this tale; most models are aware of their less than perfect aspects, so it is not unreasonable that artists seek to combine the best of many; or to phrase this the other way round, to eliminate any feature which is less than perfect.

LEMKA
(A FULL TIME PROFESSIONAL MODEL AT THE SAN CARLOS ACADEMY IN MEXICO)

He was born at the turn of the 20th century and was working regularly as an octogenarian. In the early 90's, he was given a special exhibition of the work of former students over three generations.

DORIAN GRAY
(A FICTIONAL MALE MODEL)

Oscar Wilde's novel, written in 1891, was about a male model and his portrait painted in his prime. As years went by, the aging process was transferred to the painting while the model remained a cupid-lipped Adonis – outwardly perfect despite a life of debauchery encouraged by his wicked patron and seducer, Lord Henry. The story is of little interest to the history of models other than that it depicts the social scene a century ago; when pretty boys could find social advancement via the podium in art classes. Whether Dorian posed at the Heatherley or other studios such as the Royal Academy or College is an irrelevant unknown. Not much more is known of Oscar's own research into the life school background. He would probably have been aware of the Dublin schools in his youth, where law students and soldiers in need of a few shillings were employed as models.

CELIA GREEN

The Daily Telegraph gave an obituary in 2003 to the favourite model of Sir William Russell Flint. She was his ideal physique and muse. She had been trained as a ballet dancer but after contracting TB she no longer had the stamina and decided to seek work as an artist's model. She called on Wm R-F, with whom she had a chaste relationship for many years. When she left to marry, this upset him. However, in his will she was left the contents of his studio. She often lectured on his work and exhibited his pallet and brushes. She was herself an accomplished painter.

INTERNATIONALLY FAMOUS LECTURERS ON BEING A MODEL
Two models whose life stories were of such interest that they give lectures on their careers are Celia Green, who inherited Sir William Russell Flint's studio contents, and Lydia Corbett, aka Sylvette David, alias the Girl with the Pony Tail. For she was the inspiration for Picassos' statue of that name.

Celia was a ballerina who had an accident which ended that career. Someone suggested that Flint was looking for models of her physique. So she applied and visited his studio. He stared at her with astonishment for hers was the living image of the body he had been painting in water colour for many months. That started a long relationship. Russell-Flint's work fetches high prices (£6,000 for a print and £25K for a painting) and often features unclothed women in ancient buildings/beaches, not the studio in which the figures were modelled.

Sylvette's father was an art dealer who took his family to the village in the Alps where Picasso also had taken himself to get away from the war into rustication. Sylvette had a boyfriend who she married, Corbett. She is bilingual and has homes in both France and Devon. Picasso saw her in a café and invited her to pose. Although he was clearly very attracted to her, she resisted his advances. It was her hair style and neck which particularly interested him.

OLIVIER FERNANDE
One of Picasso's early models, later his mistress, became a figure in his Demoiselles d' Avignon. It is a most unflattering work which was a huge canvas now in New York of five women of no particular good looks or physique whose angular semi-naked forms create a sharp angular image of prostitution. It was painted in Montmartre and sold to please his then 'lady' who disliked it as a depiction of Pablo's former love life. The studio atelier then used by Picasso in his effort to out do Matisse and those who sought to modernise painting was Bateau de Lavoir, which means 'wash-house'.

LA FORINARINA

Raphael, the great Italian painter whose name is linked to Leonardo and Michelangelo as the three great men of the renaissance art, died aged thirty-six. His career began when he was seventeen in 1500 – his father also a court painter and architect to Urbino, who died when he was eleven. His great speciality was to reveal the character and psychological make-up of his patrons.

Raphael is buried next to his fiancée, the niece of a cardinal whose portrait is well known for the splendid red robe he wears. In 2000, the portrait of an almost nude woman 'La Forinarina', alias Margherina Luti, in the Barberini Palace, Rome, was found to be by his hand, it had previously been thought to be by his assistant Romana. The model was the baker's daughter, who was also his mistress. He is said to have died of excessive libido – perhaps associated more with the subject of the painting than with the presumably virginal lady buried beside him.

In the same page of the Daily Telegraph as the previous item was a nude photo of the Yves St Laurent poster advert for OPIUM which was banned by the Advertising Standards Authority. Sophie Dahl, grand-daughter of the author R. Dahl, wearing only a necklace, a bracelet and high-heeled sandal, was deemed too offensive and sexually suggestive – having attracted over 700 complaints

This contrasts the attitudes over the centuries with nudity at least of males being an honour – so the list ends with:

EMPEROR HONORIUS

Mosaics showing him in the heroic nude pose with clad wife and generals in armour exist. He was a 5th Century AD Byzantine considered to be of apostolic stature, in theological terms. As such, he is the most important person in a group, his victor supreme status marked by his naked splendour – quite the reverse of later attitudes, where the vanquished are paraded naked before the Roman emperors.

HON JOHN COLLIER OBE.

Although models are rarely expected to pose with any but inanimate objects, snakes featured for two reasons in several of the Victorian 'new woman' work.

Circa 1997, both Rosetti and the Hon John Collier O.B.E. worked on the legend of Lilith, who in Talmudic tradition was the first wife of Adam. She was the ultimate femme fatale seeking her lover, the serpent, in order to revenge herself on pregnant women and children.

The athlete wrestling the serpent is of Herculean tradition, only in part. But who knows what notions of psychological mystery were involved.

Collier's first wife was also a painter of the nude; she died in childbirth, in 1887, soon after her husband had finished his Lilith. His father was the lawyer/judge First Baron Monkswell QC, an amateur painter, who clearly did not seen nude painting as pornographic. Marian and Ethel, his second wife, were sisters, daughters of the celebrated scientist Sir T.H. Huxley FRS, Clearly, a century ago, the process of liberation for women had begun in the Life studio for the daughters of the educated classes.

LORD NEWRY, ALIAS HON FRANCIS NEEDHAM – ACHILLES

A statue of Achilles was erected in 1822 as a tribute to the Duke of Wellington. It was funded by subscriptions from 'the Women of England'. The model was said to have been Francis Jack Needham born 1787, the second Earl of Kilmorey. He was also a 13th Viscount ca. 1625. The family trace themselves to the Nedehams of Cheshire since the 12th Century; they had moved to Ireland as a part of the plantation of Queen Elizabeth. Known as 'Black Jack', he was buried in 1867 in the mausoleum he had built for his teenage mistress in Twickenham. These dates are of interest in relation to attitudes to nudity and morality. He had married in 1814 and his heir was born a year later.

In 1873, Giacoimo Favretto painted 'The Anatomy Lesson' in Gall. Mod. Art, Milan. It shows a group of students with a plaster cast of a nude male. It is said that this shows/exposes 'academic art' as clinging to long lost formulae. In an age when the teaching of structural anatomy could not use live models as these were considered to be scandalous. So Lord Francis N., courtesy titled Viscount Newry as he was then styled, was something of a new pioneer, if the story is true.

CHARLES ESTAMPES VALENCAY

Few know that it was a French aristocrat who introduced life drawing to Ireland. He was General Charles Valencay FRS LLD MRIA, a Huguenot refugee protestant, a polymath. The family name was Estampes; his mother was related to the French King's ambassador, Barillon, to King James II. He had been adopted by a bachelor Scottish general, an 'uncle'.

After the revocation of the Edict of Nantes and expulsion from France, CV was educated at Eton, then Woolwich. He was trained as a military engineer and made the first modern map of Ireland. He translated French military papers into English, studied ancient dead languages, mineralogy and chemistry.

He also attempted an Irish< >English dictionary. He was a polymath – knowledgeable on many subjects and mocked for his errors. His biography is in many reference books, but few mention his interest in drawing.

He organised, in retirement, the first life classes to be held in Ireland at the Royal Dublin Society for training the skilled craftsmen who made plasterwork, sculptures and artefacts for grand mansions. He imported the principles of life drawing from Paris to Dublin, where he went on a visit to recover an earlier Survey of Ireland, lost in a sea battle.

It is known that an impoverished law student and soldiers became the models. As a senior British officer and heir to three French marquisates, he seems to have had diplomatic privilege. His family home in France had been expropriated to become the home of Tallyrand, Prince Bishop of Perigord, the great survivor finance minister to both Napoleon and both Kings Louis. Tallyrand was said to be the father of Delacroix [of the cross].

VAN EYK – MISS

Miss van Eyk was the pioneer/originator of the Register of Artists' Models. She had been a model in London pre-war 1938-ish. In the 70's, she began to organise models for various schools and courses on a roster, able to contact a variety of her former colleagues. She relied on the telephone to organise jobs for models. When she retired, her mantle fell on the founder of RAM – her successor www.Modelreg.com.

She was most insistent upon propriety, punctuality, reliability, good manners and speech: and proper respect being shown to her clients. She had a story of some 'posh' girl student who had asked her to get her a cup of tea in a break.

"Models get their own tea" was the response.

This was her motivation to better the lot of all models, of which this book is a small part.

Cecil Collins

Any discussion of the place of life drawing in English art education would be incomplete without mention of the role of Cecil Collins, who taught in Southern England at the end of the 20th Century. He resisted the sneers of his modernist colleagues who regarded the old school of short poses, of from minutes to hours, as useless and outmoded.

The Slade and other major London schools, at that time used poses lasting for months. All students at the former were required to make exact figurative drawings of the whole body. They started with marks to denote key locations, with great accuracy, corrected over long periods of weeks. Their drawings were covered with the school's hall-mark of fine x + and dots. Only when the tutor was satisfied that every mark was on exactly the correct place on the paper was any semblance of a line drawing started. This took aeons and exasperated many who did not realise that genius is the capacity to take infinite pains over detail.

Despite ridicule, Collins, abandoned this approach but persisted with life classes as a vehicle for making students observe, see and understand that most complex subject, the human figure.

Collins rejected the old discipline and allowed his students far greater freedom to express themselves, often without enough thought about the detail. In place of the fine pointed pencils he encouraged the use of quills, sticks and crude mark makers. His students, some of whom became disciples and felt the urge to carry on his work, have carried the torch and there are several from whom the author has been most grateful to learn the techniques, both as students of drawing and as models.

An obituary of Collins appeared in the Daily Telegraph and a memorial service was held in Winchester where he had installed stained glass windows. His paintings were often of himself in a clown's garb, in some prophetic role. He managed to defeat the more forceful and loud of his critics by quiet, calm plus the clarion support of appreciative students. Rachel Clarke holds classes based on his methods, www.rachelcarke.com. The success of the RA Lessons for Life Outreach to schools in 1994, described in the following paragraphs, is a vindication of Collins' perseverance.

LORD LEIGHTON'S 'SLUGGARD'

The posters for the Victorian nude exhibition in the Tate in 2001 featured a statue, life sized, by Lord L. It was entitled the 'Sluggard' but formerly it was known as the 'Awakening Athlete'.

The statue is 6' 3" in height or 1.91m. The 20" high maquette is to be seen in Plate 130 and also a photo of Leighton taken ca. 1891 and reproduced in plate 142 of the biography by Leonee & Richard Ormond published by the Paul Mellon Centre for Studies in British Art ISBN 0-300-01896-7.

The *Borezzo* or first stage as the Italians term the model of the model from which the final work is enlarged is less than 1/4 of the scale. But from the physiological point of view the model is of a man of ecto mesomorphic extreme and endomorphic minimum – to the point of appearing to be almost escorchée, flayed to expose the muscularity. That is very tall and linear man who was also very muscular. In Sheldon's somatotype a 0 Adiposity and the maximum 7 for the combination of linearity and muscle, and so giving great strength through leverage and height. That, it so happens, is also the somatotype of the manikin used in the illustrations in this tome. Which is itself the mannikin sold by Ikea, the Scandinavian furniture emporia who purvey good taste. The tall, thin muscular Viking.... who has the same anthropometry as Evander Holyfield, the world champion boxer. That is an 8' arm span.

Surprisingly the model Leighton used was of Italian extraction, as were male models.

He also worked from actresses. Lily Langtry, mistress of the Prince of Wales, is to be seen reclining in a revealing diaphanous garment, side view, in the Idyll, a bare-backed, muscular, flautist-shepherd on a pastoral scene.

Another actress was Leighton's favorite female model – Ada who used the *nom de pose* Dorothy Dene. She was, like Holman

Hunt's Anne Miller, a potential spouse, muse and ideal woman. Anne was the prototype Pygmalion – marriageable – but for the vowels and other attributes of origins in a lower educational and educational class than the artists. Leighton encouraged Dorothy to have elocution lessons with a view to becoming an actress and paid for her to go to Italy. She had ten siblings. Another sister was an actress model.

In Media, for example, painted in 1866-8, Emma is clutching at her throat while she blends a brew of some potion – toads and other ingredients reminiscent of Macbeth's three witches. The choking emotion is presentably in anticipation of the effect of the concoction.

In Helen of Troy he reveals the impatience and petulance of a poor little rich kid.

Nowadays it is unusual for models to be asked to act, as well as to pose.

PETTIGEW FAMILY OF THREE SISTERS

The three sisters Pettigrew were models for T. Roussel, Whistler and others. Henrietta Sleina, the eldest of the three sisters, was a sculptress and can be seen in her prime ca 1886 as the Girl reading an oil on canvas about five feet square. She was the artist's mistress and had born his one year old when the painting was done.

She was born in 1867 – so was aged twenty. She died in 1953. When Roussel's wife died in 1914, unexpectedly he did not marry her but instead wed a widow. Caveat – it seems some artists prefer their models to be their mistresses.

Lily Pettigrew posed for photographers such as Edward Sambourne – in 1889 August till in her prime (see fig 92v in the Victorian Nude). She was also photographed by Maud Easston at the same period. She had the same physique of a somatotype 444 – average muscularity, linearity and plumpness.

THE 3 DENE SISTERS

Ellen, married the artist Herbed Schmalz in 1888 Dorothy Dene was painted by GF Watts and had the androgynous physique which allowed the body to undergo sex-changes at the whim of the artist The 'Dane sisters', all neé Pullan, were Dorothy, Edith, Hetty and

Kathleen (who was wilds They were left a death-bed legacy/trust by Leighton.

MURIEL SPARKS

A book which inspired this section on famous models is 'Dolly on the Dais' by Muriel Segal (co-author Iris Furlong) sub-titled 'the Mist's model in perspective' by Gentry Books 1972. The authoress, an Australian American, was a former art student turned journalist. So it is written in a readable style, neither too academic nor too learned but with plenty of good material. There is little mention of male models, other than tales of jealous boys who tried to sabotage their Greek patrons' interest in pryneis; this word came to mean model in French, but comes from a Greek word meaning sieve alluding to the way my in which model-mistresses milked the coins from their patron's pockets. Unheard of in 2005 when 37% of artists earn under £5,000 p.a., vice versa more likely.

Muriel Sparks' theme can be gauged by the colours of the paper and ink – from memory, green and purple, and the collage of naked ladies on the dust cover. It is aimed at a readership interested in tittle-tattle about the morals of the famous.

MICHAEL LAW (HENRIETTA MOREAS' FIRST HUSBAND)

A clergyman's son who was married to H.M. in 1952, a year after they had met. She was a teenager newly arrived in Soho – then called Wendy Welling, from Northants. He was a thirty-five-year-old, then married to the actress dancer Maria Barry, who divorced him for his affair with Wendy who he renamed Henrietta – after his first girlfriend. Michael had brought her to a studio as a potential model. He had been educated in Westminster and Paris Univ. He later specialised in film-making cinema in Wardour Street. He had been an art student under Henry Moore and Graham Sutherland at Chelsea. His mother had moved there as a divorcee, moving in artistic circles including Sir William Orpen and Augustus John – so Law was very well connected and very good-looking.

---

* This is a technique used by Rodin in his well known portrait of Balzac. Under the cloak is a portly nude, but only the face is visible.

But he was a preoccupied, chronic womaniser, handsome and very attractive to women. She was then modelling for Lucien Freud and had consummated that relationship in a basement kitchen in Brewer Street. She left both for the body-builder Norman Bowler, who was also lover of John Minton , a painter. More of her life elsewhere. He married again in 1960 [see obit DT 20xii2001 Ip23.]

Michael Law (1917-2001).

FREDERICK SANDYS 1829-1904

The Pre-Raphaelite Brotherhood – Rossetti, Millais, etc – more often than not used their female 'sisterhood' as models for their greater works.

Fred Sandys was a late arrival to their circle, being introduced by Rossetti who was amused at his spoof-cartoon mocking Sir John Millais, was the young son of a painter in Norwich. He had been taught to paint by George Richmond and the better known Sir Thomas Lawrence, whose technique the young Fred mastered to the extent that his early works were likened to Ingres and David.

On arrival in London, in his thirties, he already had a mistress and common law wife, The latter was the actress Mary Emma Jones, the former a gipsy named Keomi. Both were models. They were required to express some emotion while posing rather than the rather bland looks depicted by the other PRB.

BRIDGET WOODS

A recently published book on 'Life Drawing' by Bridget Woods, who teaches in several colleges on the south coast, was reviewed in the Artist May 2004 and later, in March 2005, it was published by Crowood Press [ISBN 1-86126-598-0] Details can be found on the web from

www.artistsandauthors.co.uk/bridgetwoods

Her approach to models – she recommends RAM members – is modern and enlightened. As also are her teaching methods; for example an exercise of draping a sheet over the model* to show the lines connecting the knees, elbows, crown, feet, hips

---

** Three were over 60 – one was 87! All were delighted at the words above.

and how these can be used as a framework of triangles in a multi-pointed star as a start to any drawing. Many beginners fail to see the whole pose and concentrate too soon on the line detail, whereas the major relationships of the triangulation of the whole pose is paramount.

Her reviewer suggested that the models in the illustrations, while young** lithe and flexible, lacked variety – for they should be 'liquorice allsorts' – all shapes/sizes/colours/ages. Sadly, not all are available in the south so Bridget had to draw from the palette/pool of models available.

BELLA

'Bella' is a lay figure to be seen in Packwood House, a National Trust property south east of Birmingham. She was owned by Mr. Baron Ash who left his fine restored properties to the NT having furnished them for houses in the vicinity. One nearby was owned by Ms. Dering, an amateur painter, who used 'Bella' to wear the clothes after the living portrait subject's face was finished and the model departed.

She was life sized and padded with sophisticated ball and socket joints which allowed her to assume any posture. She had human hair and was painted with realistic make-up. She was probably made in Paris in the mid 19th C. She sat in a sedan chair. Pre-20th C history is unknown.

The term 'lay figure' comes from the Dutch word lede, meaning jointed. While lay figures do not move/talk/need rest or make eye-contact with the artists, thus exhibiting none of the undesirable features in a live life model, they are no more than the hangers on which to support fabric textiles [a clothes horse].

Models need not fear competition from such as they lack a range of physique – Rodin, for example, made a nude model of Balzac before he draped it in a cloak.

Life models may find themselves asked to pose nude before wearing garments, possibly for an eminent third party's clothed portrait. Models can take heart from the notion that the Canova statue of Napoleon clad in a fig leaf is now in the Duke of Wellington's London home. He may have relied on a look-alike stand-in.

XL-Y FRONTS

Michelangelo's painting in the dome of St Peter's, Rome, is well known. The artist, who was a protégé of the Medici family, painted the scenes of hoards of nudes at the Pope's request. They were all totally naked. But later, when the Medicis fell from grace, new popes and the more prudish cardinals ordered that the naughty bits be covered. The name of the artist who executed the drapery is known but he was nick-named the Italian for 'outsized Y fronts', alias *big drawers*. This explanation achieves better ambiguity when told in English – a pun on the ambiguity of the word *drawers*. A paradox about modern life classes is that those drawing are essential while drawers as garments are a sign of outmoded prudery; chests of drawers are optional.

VENUES

In most jobs it is possible to describe the places [venues] where the work will be done. A forge for a blacksmith; an operating theatre for a nurse or brain surgeon.

But for an artists' model a studio[1] – what is that like?

The life drawing studios of Rowlandson's day in the Royal Academy exist today just as they were then used for the same purpose. So do those in Paris and San Carlos in Mexico. But the average new model for life classes in 2000 may well be posing in venues or locations such as:

Art Galleries, either after hours or even during them such as the Van Gogh in Amsterdam on Sunday mornings; others such as the Mall Gallery in London have several models for many pre-booked sessions in the evenings. The Study Gallery in Poole is an ideal venue and much appreciated.

Prefabricated hut – formerly a school class room, with windows looking onto playing fields.

A shop-front window – whitened out to obscure the view into the High Street.

---

[1] STUDIO DEFINITION: A studio is an arena where groups meet to improve their self-awareness, though ART.

According to Dr Sam Johnson **ART** is *"the power of doing something not taught by nature or instinct... as to walk is natural but to dance is an art"*.

An academy which derives from a Latin word derived from a Greek word, is *"an assembly of men uniting in the promotion of some ART"*.

<u>Church halls</u> – many, of several denominations, welcome artists.

<u>Fire stations</u> – in London and at the seaside.

<u>The Girl Guides' HQ Hall</u> – in the New Forest.

<u>A former Thameside school</u> in West Chelsea – Heatherley.

<u>A former Magistrates' Court.</u>

<u>A former school gym</u> – which had splendid ceiling height.

<u>Swimming-pools</u> – both public and private.

<u>Castle Moat.</u>

<u>Hotel bars, cafes and restaurants.</u>

<u>A London lunch bar</u> – 'The Artist and Palette' in the '60s in which diners and artists drew nourishment.

<u>Attic studios</u> – with spaces for six artists at the most.

<u>Former stables and milking parlours.</u>

<u>A former night club discotheque</u> – Chapdeuil, Dordogne.

AND of course many <u>purpose-built life drawing studios</u> with spaces for twenty-plus easels. Some are the worst adapted for the purposes of artists and are poorly designed from the models' point of view.

Others, such as the Albany in Edmonton, Alberta, the 27th floor, penthouse of a high-rise was designed by the architects O'Connor to be a studio. It was nigh perfect.

One of a very few properly equipped UK studios is to be found in the Royal College of Art. It was purpose built for Prof. B Neale RA. Unique, or almost so, is its provision of stairs, mirrors, visible clocks and means of giving backgrounds of white and black, and simple sliding doors. It has huge daylight windows and instant curtaining. But the plumbing is not nearby, nor are the changing facilities secure.

Life studios are one of the oldest, rather than the youngest, educational buildings to need specially designed space they are, more often than not, moved from pillar to post within sub-average class rooms. An exception is the Royal College of Art in Kensington opposite the Albert Memorial, London. Another is the Academie Grande Chaumier in Paris, described below.

The RCA has a specially designed huge window, north facing: shading via full curtains, and behind this several floor levels with a dias and background, as in a theatre.

It is more usual to have a **life** class in some otherwise disused area, an attic or picture gallery as in some of the figures, in a classroom with windows masked temporarily with paper or net curtains. A shop-window of a cafe was once used with white-wash/greenhouse white to prevent those on the street outside observing the nude model, inside.

In London there was in the '60s a restaurant, the 'Brush and Pallet', where the tables for meals were served by waiters and waitresses while artists painted and drew from nude models in various poses in a 'floor-show' which attracted a bohemian clientele.

By contrast, church halls are often used as life studios. The hours available suit the different clienteles' needs. It is often a surprise to the prudish that the reverend incumbents rarely see anything in the least wrong about nudity on church premises. They are more open-minded than some of the non-believers. When asked if he had any objection to a life model, one had a comical way of giving his permission – he referred to the condition as LIVE (= the opposite of dead) as in the strip-club bars of the seedier parts of most cities – 'Live Models', in winking red-lights, means the opposite of celluloid.

The Heatherley open studio, formerly in Warwick Square near Victoria, London, now in a former school a few miles up-stream, has managed to make reasonable studios from class room and gymnasium spaces. Gyms often have suitable bars and mirrors. So too do rehearsal rooms associated with stages.

In south-west France, a former night-club/discotheque is now a gallery and is used once a week as a life studio. The dance floor is an excellent central feature for the model.

Many galleries of both varieties – sales and exhibition, have models and spaces in open-studios or pre-booked courses, after closing time – including the Mall Gallery, off Birdcage Walk in London; in Amsterdam – the Van Gogh; and ArtSway in the New Forest. For both models and artists a good way of finding studios is to ask at the local art materials shop – often called a gallery.

The moat of a castle, several swimming pools, two former fire-station and a gymnasium (very apt for the Greek word *gymnos* means nude) are amongst the unlikely venues for which part-time models are sought.

The Mall Galleries are the focus of much of the life drawing in England.

They are the administrative centre of the Hesketh Hubbard Art Society, which was formed out of the former RBA (Royal Society of British Artists) in 1953. The Mall Galleries also host many organisations such as the FBA (Federation of British Artists) and the NEAC (New England Art Club). These should not be confused with the RSA (Royal Society of Arts) which is 250 years old and encourages art in commerce, manufacture, etc, which is in John Adam Street.

Just as the Grande Chaumier is in Montparnasse, the Paris district of many artistic activities, so the Mall Galleries are near the National Galleries in Trafalgar Square, central London. The address is: 17 Carlton House Terrace, London, SW1 5DB; 0207 930 6844; www.mallgalleries.org.uk

There are two-hour evening Life sessions once per week where models – one for portrait and two for Life – pose, in both long and short poses. The full-year subscription is very reasonable.

The Grande Chaumier, means the Big Thatched House, is across the square from Vavin Metro Station. A one star *Hotel Academie* is in the opposite side of the Rue Gde Chaum. Also, there is a Great Western Hotel opposite.

The owner/founder was a Mr Carpentier whose teaching academy is nearby. It is open to the public on payment of a fee (ca. £10 a session) 0900-1700 hours Monday-Saturday. The mornings are for painters with long poses, afternoons are for drawing. There is a roster of ca. 30 models who are mainly female. Male models are available on the first and third Wednesdays of the month.

There is a strict formula for rest and length of poses. The model takes a short break to relieve cramp, etc. at will. The last hour is for five-minute poses broken into two 25-minute slots with a five-minute rest break. The earlier afternoon is a 45-minute pose for the first hour, with 15 minutes break. Then, three half-hour poses with five/ten minute breaks. The exact times are displayed on a wall opposite the studio clock, above the entrance door. There are spaces for 30 artists. Some felt that the sessions should begin with 'warm-up' short poses, as elsewhere.

The building has an impressive portico entrance with a concierge's room for payment inside the street door. The life studio is of classic design. It is two floors high with a vast glass window as the north side. The main floor is about 8m x 15m arranged with three tiers of spaces with a four row under the window facing the model's podium, about a metre above the lowest tier. A waist-height banister rail keeps the rows of spaces apart to prevent easel-dropping.

Above the entry door next to the *guardien's bureau* is a gallery with a stair open to the studio. There is the opportunity for artists to find various aspects/angles from which to draw. The podium has a backdrop curtain arrangement for easy changes. There is a large mirror next to the door. A canopy above the podium keeps the air from rising above the model. A huge cylindrical stove heats the main area in winter while the high ceiling keeps the air cool and unstuffy in hotter weather. There are three spotlights above the model and a radiant heater. The artists' area is lit by two huge cartwheel chandeliers with modern spotlights aimed at the drawing spaces. All are either on or off, which is less than ideal. A possible improvement might be individual control by means of pull-string switches. These could also be useful as sight-line aids; few others could be seen.

Email: acacharp@club-internet.fr
Website: www.grandechaumier.fr

14 rue de la Grande Chaumiere, 75006 Paris, France
01 43 26 13 72
01 43 26 66 44

Hotel de la Academie: 01 43 26 66 44

*Rowlandson's cartoon of the Life room in the Royal Academy – reproduced by
their kind permission.
This can be contrasted with a painting of the same subject in the Royal
Collection by Zoffany in 1771.*

*Note the hour glass for keeping check on the time – essential for both model and
artist, who should record the minutes for each sketch.*

*Note also the source of illumination which was both a source of heat and
shadow casting.*

*The seats bear a remarkable likeness to those carried on the backs of the model
in Loads – stone?*

Note also the carafe and liquid – wine or water?

OVERHEARD IN A STUDIO

Notice found in a laundromat/washateria
PLEASE REMOVE ALL YOUR CLOTHES WHEN THE LIGHTS GO OUT

After WWII a former life class instructor returned with new ideas about Life. He had been a much decorated fighter pilot. His family owned a household name product. He decided that his students should be asked to take all their clothes off, in a darkened studio and explore the human body by touch. Most enjoyed the experience but word got to the authorities who disapproved.

ARCHITECTS

Life studios are the architectural Cinderellas of the education world.

Some architects clearly needed to know that a NORTH light is desirable; as are windows which obscure the sights within from outsiders. Rarely are there mirrors or changeable backgrounds, or props to support the model's limbs.

The changing rooms for models are usually an afterthought. One wonders how some architects are taught art and drawing.

In one 'institute', whose designers provided no north light; arranged the windows so that the podium was visible from the main entrance door, a floor below; the roof sloped so that 20% of the floor space, behind the students, was below kneeling height, and so on.... Instead of a gallery it had empty beams into which all heat ascended. Instead of light for the students, all was on the model; as the eaves joined walls a few feet above the wainscot, this prevented tutors walking behind their students; artists need to standing back to see their work from a distance of six feet. This latter is essential, yet forgotten by the builder. After a year it was decided that this studio, opened by a HRH in 1990, needed a changing room for models; so a mini-hutch with shower was added. A screen would have sufficed!

A few miles from the institute is a public [i.e. private – fee-paying] school. It built a new arts block life studio, on a limited budget. It had a stair, at first sight, far too wide for access to a mere gallery but designed wisely as a 'prop'; artists could look down on the model, or the model could pose above them thus providing a full variety of levels to separate the subject from the model.

Any educated architect should be aware that Mantagna and many others usually drew grand scenes from a grovelling vantage point. Also that it is traditional that athletic students mount onto the beams to get unusual downward views of the model.

A view of an empty studio used daily for life-drawing by foundation students at an Art College. Note the chairs and easels, absence of much in the way of facilities for the model.

The seating is for the students rather than the model.

FIRE ALARM

It was on a cold January night in northern Canada where the studio was on the 27th floor of a hi-riser; it was twenty degrees BELOW, the need to keep a quick exit strategy became evident. The smoke reached the penthouse studio just as the alarm went off; then the lights went off. No power/no elevator/no light.

The cold concrete flights of steps was the only exit. The model was able to find her boots but her clothes were too complex to worry about until she hit the minus twenty outside. It was cold enough beside the lift shaft. Your reporter carried a bundle of drapes and her clothes hopefully amongst that which had been found by cigarette lighter illumination.

The ten from the studio, being the uppermost floor, were the last to be able to exit for the lower floors who were already in panic mode as their level was reached.

Some had parked cars in the basement park, under cover. Mine was in the street and it was to this the model fled for warmth. Cars can heat up quite quickly but it seemed an eternity for the model.

The lesson of routine fire-drill is important and permits a classification of models not often given much thought. A few nights earlier on the university campus during a late sitting of Faculty Council, the dean in the chair had become enraged by:

"Tell that idiot to stop ringing that BELL", only to be told that it was probably the real fire alarm. In some studios, a couple of decades later it is normal for the staff to be told if a practice drill is planned.

In one college with several life studios, and frequent drill, it was considered by students to be a good jape if the models fled in their working attire, as above. But after thought it was decided that this might be deemed evidence of exhibitionist tendencies; so less frequent pseudo arson incidents occurred.

All studios should inform the models of the routine to be followed if fire or other incident occurs.

STUDIO PROPS

Studio 'props' should include items needed for:

Keeping the model comfortable – changing area or screens, mirrors & clothes hangers, foam mattress.

A choice of chairs, stools, cushions, divan bed.

Background drapes of many colours and textures.

And padding for knees and elbows against hard furniture and floors.

For essential warmth – heaters rugs and mats.

Illumination = suitable spotlights and adjustable lamps.

Support for limbs – to keep difficult poses static.

Ceiling fixture to support ropes and items hung on string as sight-lines.

Boxes of various heights to form a podium.

Broom-stick, walking stick, hoops, loops of rope.

Brush and dustpan.

Quoit or tennis ball to throw to a model for a spontaneous action pose.

Blocks of foam plastic or rubber to act as padding or to simulate heavy boxes/stones being lifted/carried. Styrofoam blocks.

Ladders/steps/poles/broom-handles/umbrella or parasol to mask lights.

Visible accurate clock plus egg-timer/hour-glass. An egg timer is good for short poses although counting slowly for each second is best.

A black-board to show the duration of the pose.

Means of keeping intruders at bay = net curtains, notices.

Chalk and masking-tape to mark the pose.

First aid kit.

Telephone, 'all mobiles to be switched-off' sign.

Fire exit.

OVERHEARD IN A STUDIO

It is said there are three items that should never be taken on a yachting holiday – a ladder, an umbrella and a Commander RNVR (naval officer).

But TWO ARE ESSENTIAL IN A STUDIO – guess which.

OVERHEARD IN A STUDIO

While the artist was mixing rose madder,
The model ascended a ladder
And assumed a position
Suggesting coition
So he nipped up the ladder
and adder.

SIGHT-LINES

Definition: sight-lines are a means of ensuring that the position of the model's eyes and head remain in the same position in space while they pose. If the feet are also marked then there is less chance of the pose altering substantially, after rest breaks.

The main duty of models is to keep as **still** as they can. For normal human beings this is not natural so some help is needed. Fidgeting is unacceptable but it is something that adults can usually control: even so after ten minutes, which at first can seem an eternity, a model may slump or sag into an ungainly pose, and more critically, move within the surroundings, which students may be using for their sketch.

In seated or standing poses which may last for over fifteen minutes, it is best for the instructor to make a chalk mark around the feet and hands onto whatever supports the model, so that the pose can be resumed after a rest break, as exactly as possible. The models cannot do this for themselves, not having eyes in the backs of their heads. The head is another matter, it can be fixed is space with great accuracy by using **sight-lines**.

Once a pose is set, only the model can see SIGHT-LINES. (This is a copyright term of the author's invention). It describes the best and only way in which models can keep their heads in exactly the same place. This is achieved by taking observations of two nearby objects in space, and aligning these in BOTH vertical and horizontal planes with two other objects, one nearby the other far off. These pairs should preferably be at 45° to 90° horizontally. Also vertically. One of the pair for the left eye; the other for the right eye.

The model must first adopt the pose the artists and the instructor desire, then seek some sight-lines so that the eyes may be kept exactly where the pose began. Drooping begins with the neck. Using sight-lines entails occasional checking, one line with the right eye and the other with the left eye. The difficulty is that each sight-line must be for only one eye. As there can be a danger of a sight-line mark being moved, a prudent model will start with at least one extra pair of markers. One must avoid using the top of an easel which may be moved or a window which may be closed or lights in far off buildings which may be turned off.

A sight-line may be a mark with a grease pencil on a windowpane or on a mirror aligned with, say, a chimney pot on the other side of the road, another at 90°, in the other direction, say a mark on a lampshade in line with a cornice or a mark on the ceiling of the room. Most studios are ill-provided with such interior objects, which cannot be moved. Studios without suspended weights in strings from the ceiling lack true perpendicular and reveal the mindset of the organizers. Tiling, bricks and grids on walls usually have a dreary uniformity where a few coloured blobs of randomly spotted marks will allow the model a good choice of readily identifiable and distinguishable spots to line up with, say, a dangling weight on a string close to the podium. Often there are grids so that students can observe and measure the planes behind the model. It is helpful to the model to have some marks on the walls and a few short ropes looped to 'sky-hooks' dangling from the ceiling, to support their hands.

Studios without plenty of choices of marker for sight-lines ought to provide them. Their absence is a sure sign that those who set the poses need to pay more attention to their models' needs. No principal or head can be excused, for this or any other failure to consider their employees' needs – even if their subject is not drawing.

Mirrors can be especially useful for fixing sight-lines. A tile mirror of fifteen by fifteen centimetres is large enough, although the bigger the better. With a greased pencil coloured marks on its centre, etc, it can be moved into the model's view and adjusted, after the pose has been selected, to fix onto some point behind the model. A mirror adds to the distance of the alignment and the further away the point the more accurate the fix; also the wider an angle between the pairs of lines the better.

A spin-off of using sight-lines is that the model will gaze at some far-off object and so avoid looking at the artists who may be staring at, and even feeling, a nude body. The model, by using sight-lines, also avoids direct eye contact which can distract new persons/students unused to feeling as they look.

John Meaker's Cage *alias* Space Frame

Equipment in a studio is rarely constructed with the model in mind. Some studios have wooden frames and padded supports resembling the corner of a ring for a boxer. That is an L-shaped very, very big book-end. Several tutors have wooden frames of mini 'phone box dimensions for use in studios to enclose a model. Below is a description of a superior design.

In 2003 a portable cage was made by a female blacksmith in Bridport for a tutor, John Meaker, for his peripatetic life classes. It can be dismantled to fit into a car boot. It is a simple device to allow the model to be seen within and in close proximity to, vertical and horizontal lines. These are also very useful to ensure the model remains static and both model and the students all keep their eyes in the same relative positions to each other and the surrounds. The bars on the frame act as close-up sight-lines. The design has the advantage of providing the model with a choice of various heights of supports for feet and hands .

The frame is made of metre-long lengths of half inch square iron tubing. The box shape gives strength against bending. When assembled, it forms a mini-phone-box of ca. 4ft x 5ft x 6ft. One side is void but the other three have horizontal bars which allow the model to find suitably high supports for feet and arms so that for a variety of poses, the duration can be prolonged. The matt-black paint ensures it's presence is neither obtrusive nor reflective. Additional string can be added to make a measuring device matrix/grid available to all those drawing. Foam insulation, as used for water pipes, ensures that the model does not lose heat by conduction. It is not possible to hold an iron frame for any prolonged period without pain! Pain indicates danger.

From the model's point of view it provides plenty of nearby marks for sight-lines to ensure the eyes and head remain in a fixed position.

And from the student's each has a choice of a grid of static verticals and horizontals to include in their attempts to establish the geometry of the pose so that perspective may be perceived and measured.

MANIKINS AND LAY FIGURES – NON-PERSONS

There are several types and sizes of manikins; some are new-modern others are antique [very old]. That illustrated as a ghost is an antique from the studio of a tutor in life classes. It is an heirloom, over a century old and as the chair reveals it is about half scale. It has a patina making it dark tan. The head seems rather large for the legs, the abdomen is in proportion with the arms. It is not free standing. The legs which are not in view are out of proportion being too long!

The smaller manikins sold in art shops are about 1/6th life size and have the reverse characteristics – pale, thin, in proportion and self supporting; they can be adjusted to hold any pose defying the need for rest or a sky hook, in any possible pose and many which are impossible. They are usually made from beech wood with hinged joints.

The lay figure Bella described under 'famous persons' is life sized but cannot hold a pose without support – a chair, etc. Sickert was given a life size wooden lay-figure by his brother-in-law Major Lessore, said to have belonged to Hogarth. It is exhibited with Sickert's work – 2005 Southampton Municipal Gallery.

The antique half scale is about three feet in height; the others are only twelve inches – 1/6th scale.

The smaller manikin is of a very tall, very thin Caucasian. It could not, even if painted black, substitute for other physique or ethnic group. Herein lies one reason/explanation of a fundamental need for both live models and also manikins, of all physiques/races/sexes/ages.

Manikins can serve several useful purposes in a life studio:
1.   To show the model the approximate pose required.

2.   For the students/artists to copy the pose and to observe it from various angles.

3.   For artists to feel the pose and observe its feasibility and stressfulness.

4.   As a poor substitute for a live model.

The first use, while obviously interesting, is rare; probably because few tutors know it.

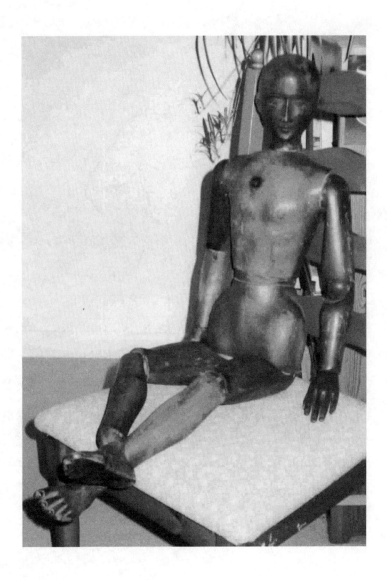

This pose is of infinite duration!
The pose is typical of standing poses hand on hip and feet apart.
It lacks any twist to provide interest and challenge to depict - other than the evident end of life pose pun.
A pose such as this could be held for a full day with suitable breaks.
It is revealed in the Devil's Dictionary that no one ever saw a nude ghost.

GHOST NU

It is revealed in the Devil's Dictionary that no one ever saw a nude ghost.

It seems that these manifestations are confined to the textiles once in close proximity to the ethereal being. It is the fabric which has substance. The shroud, the normal everyday habit which assume their former optical qualities in space, but not tangibility. Life models are sometimes covered in a sheet to accentuate the relationships between the boney parts (elbow/knee/head/feet, etc). This encourages the student to see the whole figure rather than the details of hand face without setting them into the correct place on the paper in relation to the whole figure

This may or may not be of some consolation to life models. They are, so it seems, as unlikely as bathers to haunt. No one has yet heard and reported a sighting of a ghostly swimmer, not even a non-skinny dipper. A possible reason is that their costumes were so wet that the miniscule particles which absorb the Dieing Body's radiation cannot release it.

The moral of the story may be that it is not so much the bell and candle which can cause spirits to rest but the splashing of water.

Life models are urged to contemplate whether or not to die with their boots and /or working garments : or to be assured of a better chance of peace by expiring in their working non-garb in a bath.

There is an apocryphal tale about an aged lady Russian model in communist Moscow, who posed regularly always seated sometimes snoring. She seemed to be able to remain without movement for hours. At the end of her last session someone went to awaken her – to find that she was very, very cold. No one had noticed.

LIFE AND DEATH

In pre-19th Century, public execution and amputation were common. The term operating theatre implies this dramatic spectacle to be witnessed. The public were expected to witness the spectacle. The surgeon was gauged according to the speed of his work and the recovery of his patient. The reverse held for the gallows. The knife was used to draw and quarter; to kill slowly and butcher fast. While the French guillotine was devised by medical doctor Guillot for a speedy despatch and is a subject of many drawings and paintings, depiction of hangings does not seem to have been as common. But a new reason for the use of the term Life drawing may come from a talk on 5 January 2005, BBC 4. It was a description of Lady Elizabeth who operated a gallows in Ireland before the days of scientific and humane hanging. According to the historian at that time it was normal for artists to sketch the scene. Lady Elizabeth apparently also drew from her subjects once they were lifeless.

SECURITY: THEFT AND UNWELCOME GUESTS

In Dublin, security against intruders is controlled by porters, who man an entry door to a huge studio. The same happens in Mexico City, at the San Carlos Academy. Inside the courtyards there are many door-less life studios; most have a raised platform in the centre. Facilities for models are far from modern but attitudes are different – far less prudery.

Models, though very poorly paid, may surprisingly to administrators, carry money; as every nudist knows pocketlessness is attractive to the light-fingered. Ambiguity intended.

The Royal Academy life studio, used for two centuries, still has the original cupboards at each corner of the podium/stage in which the models hang their garments -within sight. There, two models pose simultaneously as in Mexico but rarely elsewhere.

The Old Warwick Road Studios of the Heatherley Open Studio and their new premises in the abandoned school had the model's screened booth behind the podium. So simple! No need for robes and requests (to inconsiderates) to make a pathway for the model between the easels *en route* for a break.

No matter how large or small the studio, it seems that once a student has found a space, it seems almost invariably, that it becomes a 'ppp' (personal proprietorial possession), even if it is next the door into the changing booth..

A cure for 'ppp' is to ask each artist to work on a drawing for a few minutes – then change places with another, then another, who will then finish off the work. Whose work is it? Much the same as for the masters of olde tymes – many a master painter had apprentices to do the detail

OPTICS

Illumination in studios, from all light sources, is second only to the model, in importance; the next most important factor in any description of the life studio. For drawing is a visual art. It depends on photons, the minute particles which emanate from the sun or any other highly energised process such as the filament of an electric light bulb. Candles were used in the early 18th Century life classes in London, later arc lights. The ancients relied on daylight only, e.g. the 500BC Indians used light reflected off pools of water at the entrance to the Ajanta caves to paint human forms on the ceilings.

Total darkness is the opposite of light, it is found inside deep caves or in the sky at night, where stars are pin-points of light, each a sun. A model posed at the entrance to a cavern on a sunlit hillside, becomes a perfect silhouette. That is almost impossible to recreate in a studio.

The science of the matter is that after the continuous nuclear explosion that is the sun a photon takes 8.5 minutes to reach the earth. It travels at 186 thousand miles a second, vibrating at various frequencies. We can recognise some of these as colours; others, UV & infrared, are invisible to us. When light reaches the model's skin it is reflected and a few photons reach the retina of the artist's eye. This stimulates the optic nerves which by some neuro-chemical process, transmit it to the brain. Wonderful!

Light is needed both to cause shadows on and around the model or other subject being drawn and also to view the drawing or art-work.

Normally the model is in bright light; but where the model is in near darkness, the artist must be able to see the marks made.

LIGHTING

Great care must be taken when using bright lights to provide contrast of shadows. Retinal damage can occur without the model realising that the bright light from the side has entered the eye. Never accept a pose if the model's eyes are staring towards a bright light.

HEAT AND DRAUGHTS

In any life studio, the model, as the only person present without the benefit of body heat conserving clothes, takes precedence in the choice of the temperature on the podium or posing area. Usually, at least one fan heater is provided so that area is warmer than the outer vicinity. Two sources are a minimum, one as a spare, but both should be in use so that one side does not become cold while the other cooks.

As the body becomes accustomed to losing heat to the air, without the normal benefit of insulating fabrics, the temperature gradient in the skin is adjusted, involuntarily by the central nervous system. The surface becomes cool while a few millimetres below the blood is at its usual temperature. During short breaks, of less than fifteen minutes, it is better for the model **not** to wrap-up but rather to keep the system stable. If prudishness dictates, a thin wrapper should suffice.

Some principles of heat may help. Heat rises, hot air can waft out via the window without anyone benefiting. Body heat is lost mainly via the feet and head, so a carpet to insulate the feet helps as does an IR source above the model. Note the combined heat and light in Rowlandson's cartoon of the RA School two centuries ago, (see p. 68). It was probably acetylene or gas powered – an even greater fire hazard than electric elements.

An infrared lamp is safest but it casts complementary green shadows which are only useful for certain teaching purposes.

MUSIC IN LIFE CLASSES

While the general rule is that all must be silent while a model poses, music is often a much needed stimulus. In most studios to drop a pin, let alone a drawing board or easel, would be unforgivable (though not unusual); for it might startle some, such is the concentration of minds in any serious group.

However, in informal groups usually without any tutoring instruction, music can add an extra dimension to the experience. The choice of classical sonatas or jazz is a matter of the individual choice of the organisers. Rarely does anyone object to the rhythm or tune. Even songs are acceptable, in certain circumstances. As also is dance, both more so if slow.

There is a parallel between the colour of music and the shape of the melody and the finished drawings. In music as in drawing it is the silences or missing lines which draw the reader's/viewers' minds to the expression of the pose – as seen by the artist.

In Mexico in the graduate student class of Professor Chuai, music, dance, scent, incense/joss-sticks plus lighting all contributed to the understanding of sensuality of the group poses. Here the music filled a dual need of the models to dance in step with the slow music and for the artists to become attuned to the mood.

In more simple sessions the music will provide artists with a clue to a finger-tip dance possible between the pencil and paper.

From any model's standpoint it is far less boring to hear music than the absolute silence of pencils or charcoal, etc, scratching on the surface. And the sad sighs of those who despair of ever getting a likeness of the pose.

The similarity between music and drawing in the classical sense is close. In performance, the conductor is at the centre of a group as is the model in a Life Class. Both are the focus of attention of all others. The one is static: the other mobile. One is attired and jerks as if some puppet master was in control while the static nude one only moves with permission from above.

Few take any heed of either central figure: most concentrate on the papers before them. The artists mark their blank paper while the musicians just stare at indecipherable notations and act according to some synchronised orders from outer space. One lot have immutable notes, the others change their marks constantly. Indeed, if some extra-terrestrial ET being happened upon a Life Class and a rehearsal for a concert, great puzzlement might ensue. For both are groups without any semblance of order, purpose or group dynamics. Yet all are engaged in some fascinating artistic endeavour.

SCALE AND SCALES

While it is true that art students in their early years are encouraged to draw from observation, for the sole purpose of monitoring their technical abilities and to improve their eye-hand co-ordination, this stage soon ends. Life drawing then becomes an academic discipline totally devoid of intellectual, political or philosophic consciousness. Unlike many art practices, despite the fact that it deals with one of the more controversial aspects of art, life drawing has largely managed to avoid the scrutiny and critical enquiry of historians. Here the analogy with playing the <u>scales</u> on a musical instrument is useful. Initially the purpose is to train the brain, hand, ear, eye co-ordination. Later it is to exercise, by repetition, an acquired dexterity.

Just as one recites poetry in times of stress, many models recite in silence on the podium.

Others while away the minutes by sending messages in Morse code or alpha bravo, the new phonetic alphabet.

The _scale_ of drawings is also an important variant to be practiced in a life studio.

Beginners seem to prefer very small scale as in hand-writing; the more experienced like to draw on a very large scale. For this, wallpaper liner is especially useful as a complete scroll of a series of short poses can be filed for future reference. Rolls are much more simple to transport than flat sheets of paper.

This composition of several poses of the same model, of average linearity and above average muscularity and normal adiposity, illustrates the central standing pose is more tiring (even with a broom stick across the shoulders) than those with legs astride which provide greater stability – but the upstretched arms and bent spine make them just as fatiguing so with 20% time paid for rest between stints of 30-minute stints: kneeling and crouching 20 minutes max..

MODEL *cf.* CONDUCTOR

The similarity between music and drawing in the classical sense is close.

In performance, the conductor is at the centre of a group as is the model in a Life Class. Both are the focus of attention of all others. The one is static: the other mobile.

One is attired and jerks as if some puppet master was in control while the static one only moves with permission from above.

Few take any heed of either central figure: most concentrate on the papers before them. The artists mark their blank paper while the musicians just stare at indecipherable notations and act according to some synchronised orders from outer space. One lot have immutable notes; the others change their marks constantly. Indeed if some extra-terrestrial being happened upon a life class and a rehearsal for a concert great puzzlement might ensue. For both are groups without any semblance of order, purpose or group dynamics. Yet all are engaged in some fascinating artistic endeavour.

The musicians favour the same black and white colourless garb that is the artists' choice of colour for their marks. Charcoal and paper white.

Are the visual and the audial the same in opposite ways?

OVERHEARD IN A STUDIO

The studio in question was the pent-house of a hi-rise in an oil-rich N. American city. Every Thursday at 1930 hrs a group of professionals met to draw from a model, also to drink a few glasses of wine. The group included professors, surgeons, geologists, accountants, lawyers, etc. One accomplished water-colourist Bob, an orthopaedic surgeon, well known for his skills in repairing severe fractures of skiers. He usually came from the operating theatre with such spare plastic bone as had not 'gone off' and was surplus to the needs of the patient. It was like plastic ivory – a geologist used it to make miniature sculptures. In the Japanese style. He wandered around the studio to observe from various angles while the others drew or painted. He was very polite and considerate and almost never obstructed the static artists' view.

"Dammit!" swore Bob," I have made two **new** knees this afternoon and I cannot even draw one in two dimensions tonight"

"Do you know what is the most difficult operation in the world" asked the geologist hoping to pour oil on the water. "I heard that at a recent convention of international surgeons a Russian, an American and an Englishman met to discuss that very point.

The American described a procedure in the brain which had only 5% chance of success; the Englishman described a removal of a growth on the spinal cord 6%. Then the Russian announced that the **most difficult** operation under a communist regime was the tonsilectomy. The USA and UK men were astonished. 'Our success ratio is over 99.9%. How can you kill so many?' Then the Russian growled: 'You are not understanding – in USSR we have to keep our mouths shut **at all times** so we remove the tonsils thru' the arse.'

The point in repeating this drollery is that models, in some studios, are expected to 'keep the mouth shut.' This can create an atmosphere of intense oppression. While in some teaching situations this may be necessary, in social groups Absolute silence is not always the most conducive to creative work. Bob's outburst did break the silence – but it helped to clear the air.

CATS, DOGS AND DRAWING PINS – BANNED FROM STUDIOS

Drawing pins, like cats and dogs, must be **banned** from studios where there is a life model with bare feet. In the case of cats it is not only that they may find difficulty in distinguishing between table legs and a model's static leg as a claw-sharpening challenge, but that cats and dogs cannot understand a *homo sapiens* who is immobile. They try to get attention and cannot understand why the immobile person is the focus of everyone else's fervent attention. Jealous?

Cats seek to draw attention to themselves by purring and brushing themselves against the model in the hope of getting a pat or stroke.

Some models arrive with their pet; unless very well behaved they should be asked to leave the hound or moggy outside the studio.

Drawing pins are a hazard and must be rigorously forbidden. As also must the use of fixative for charcoal or pastel within the studio. It is very dangerous if inhaled by anyone – asthmatics, especially, have reason to complain. Most studios are already 'no smoking' areas

Hair spray can be used to anaesthetise mice, especially those brought home by domesticated cats, according to a letter to the Daily Telegraph January 27, 2005. Mice should be rare in studios as only drinks, not food, should be consumed therein!

Cameras should only be allowed in studios if BOTH the model/s and organisers have given prior permission – in writing preferably.

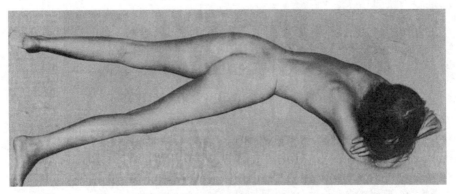

This photo, which arrived via the web, is alleged to be pre-1920.
It is included as an example of a prostrate pose which is relaxed and could
last for an hour without any break; or for longer or shorter durations - up to a
whole day, with the usual rest periods for reasons other than muscular strain.
The minimum would be twenty (+ five for changing, etc) minutes after two
hours, with five minutes 'on offer' at the end of the first half hour. The first part
of a long pose can be more difficult to hold than the later stints.
But, if it was a back view of a standing pose, which is most unlikely, then
several artists might have an opportunity to draw it simultaneously. The rest
needed would be twice that above. But if it is face down in the sand, then the
artist must have had either a balcony site; or improbably stilts or a ladder or a
crane.

POSING AND POSES?

POSING is a term which implies posturing or assuming body language stances which are exaggerated. All life models must pose; however the extent to which they overdo the interesting curvilinear and unusual aspects of the human form can be only a short step from exhibitionism. There is no place for acrobatic contortions, balancing acts or overacted character parts. Even the best and fittest will find it impossible to hold such poses for the required durations.

Tutors in life classes and others like to imagine that they can 'set an interesting pose' – RUBBISH! Only the model can decide what can and **what cannot** be held for the intended duration. The duration must be decided before the model selects props, sight-lines and comfort paddings, carpets, etc.

A secret of holding poses is to assume a very contorted position, with the hands and feet all at different levels and with the spine, neck and limbs twisted – variously. Then **relax** the twists for they will be far too fatiguing. After a minute, find where the pressure is on elbows, etc., to adjust the surfaces. The longer the pose the more the time that should be spent in getting the comfort of the model assured.

POSES

Experienced models will know how to do both short and long poses and will have a repertoire of various degrees of twisted contortions which they know can be held for both short and long durations. New students may find some of the more contorted or foreshortened difficult so the model is in some way required to understand what is needed.

113

The illustrations are intended to give some ideas. Standing, sitting, lying down, crouched, etc. Also, action poses and moving poses. In these a model may hold a pole at the centre of a circle of, say eight feet, diameter for footprints placed in the same spot on each gyration, of a very slow march. A pace every four seconds.

Action poses which have a hint of a movement arrested in mid-flight are especially needed. It helps to have a pole, broom handle and some firm hand-holds from the ceiling or walls to stabilise the more energetic poses.

A slumped pose like a sack of potatoes is rarely acceptable. The pinned-out symetrically about the spine with arms and legs in the same plane are also less interesting than a pose with a twist in the torso and neck and shoulders and hips cocked out of horizontal, the most comfortable but least artistic gestures.

In open studio sessions it is normal to 'warm-up' with a series of short standing action poses of five, seven, ten minutes; maybe one, two, three, four, five quick poses. This helps those drawing to see the model from various angles and to form a general idea before settling down to a pose of, say, twenty minutes.

The routine varies from studio to class. Some prefer to warm up with a crescendo of shorter and very short; others end a session with a few quick gesture poses after a long session of exact drawing.

Levitation which it seems might just have been contrived from a pose held while standing or lying on the back, and then the drawing inverted.
The standing figures are in poses which might last up to fifteen minutes if the fists were holding sky-hooks [ropes from ceiling].
The flying figures might have been drawn from a pose face down supported by a large cushion or a low bed.

Spearman Scalped and Ghouls - after Flaxman
The spearman is posed with various props and with his feet on two levels.
This pose might be held for about ten minutes, it is quite energetic for the
balance is vital.
The victim probably had his feet at different levels so that the right foot is about
two inches above the left. His hands, if supported by some prop, would allow
the pose to last for twenty minutes.
The winged figure despite the apparent defiance of gravity was done from a
kneeling pose possibly holding onto a rope over the right shoulder.
The other kneeling figure at the left has a much easier pose, although probably
another view of the winged, which would last only half the time.

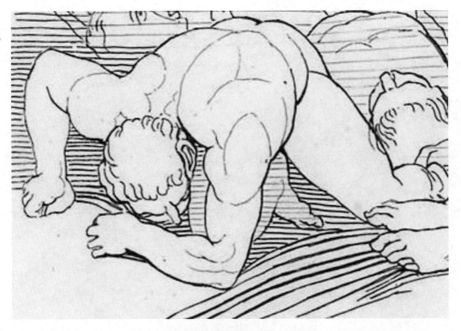

Crouching figure by Flaxman
Ten minute pose, probably good from many aspects. Could be held for fifteen minutes, if mats soften the floor pressure on knees.
This kneeling pose would be hard on the knees and arms. Fifteen minutes maximum even with soft rubber carpet pads/cushions. Then five minutes break to recover circulation.
The viewer's eye level seems to be about neck height. Is the neck possible? The head probably sagged because no sight-lines are feasible and no head/chin rest could be improvised.

Turn this page 180 degrees [upside down] and it will be apparent that the central model posed while recumbent - on his back - holding a pole. Thirty minutes with five-minute breaks would be adequate.

Although apparently a moving pose – the castanets give the illusion of finger snapping – this standing-pose could be held for many minutes, but the strain clearly falls on the hands, which would tend to sag, unless supported. In fact the model did not use such aid. It was a half hour drawing with breaks.

This part of a composition by Flaxman shows a pose very similar to that on the facing page of a more recent model at a window. The spear has replaced a window sill or other support.
The weight is unevenly distributed between the arms, and the angle is closer to forty-five degrees than the twenty-five of the model photographed. This pose could, depending on the strength of the model, in this case clearly substantial, last for about twenty minutes, before the onset of shaking. As the twist in the torso and as most of the weight is on the arms, ten-minutes pose followed by five minutes rest would be appropriate.

The model and artist with her earlier sketch from the same pose in a more upright stance. The pose lasted for two hours, with ten minute breaks every half hour, after which the spine became more vertical. The more inclined this type of pose, the greater the strain on the arms.
It lacks any 'twist' as it was an exercise in an Art College for Foundation students to encourage the accurate measurement of angles so that a realistic balance of weight was evident in their sketches.

PHYSIQUE

Physique is scientifically measurable, like many other facets of our bodies, and can also described by many more words than other phenomena. The words differ according to language. The French sometimes complain that most of their models are *jeune mince*, meaning young, thin and elegant females. They seek more older and fatter and muscular women or men as life models.

The simple 'ponderal index' of physique is the square of the height divided into the weight. It depends of the unit – metric or ancient.* From this, an indication of the need for more exercise and less food (or vice versa) is derived. Modern electronic gadgets will do the calculation for a fee, often in gymnasia

Physique is measured more scientifically from its three components ectomorphy, mesomorphy and endomorphy [linearity, muscularity and obesity in simpler terms]; the archetypal extreme cases being Twiggy, Charles Atlas, Billy Bunter. Normally, people are a mixture of all three. Each can be expressed on a scale of 1-7: the average mid-point being 4. The average normal person might be close to 444 but few exist; 353/533/335 being considered normal. The same with height. Models of over two metres are rare, as are midgets. Both are desirable in studios.

The scientific name for physique measurement is 'Somatotyping'. It is based on a system of measuring the limbs' photographic diameters and expressing these as a ratio of height: it was invented by Sheldon. His 'Atlas of Man' 1922 contains photographs of every known type of physique. 'Redintegrated Somatotyping', a computerised version, an improvement on

* e.g. a 2-metre high man of 100 kg has a 2.5 P.I.

Sheldon's subjective method was invented by Preston and Singh in Canada, and published in Photogrammetry in 1980.

It produces a curve of the body diameters from amputated silhouettes

It was found that in life classes students tend to draw models as if they were of similar physique to the artist. The fat add endomorphy; the very thin reduce the limbs' width; while the muscular add mesomorphy. While there are many body-building male models and fat female models there are few anorexics.

Part of the problem of life drawing is accurate portrayal of physique. The illustrations include some examples. Flaxman clearly used male models who were of above average muscularity, with below average ecto- and endo-morphy. There are herein sketches of a fat lady, who is 6 – above average endomorphy. The figure by the window is an extreme ectomorph, of average muscularity. Manikins sold in art shops are abnormally tall and of ectomorphic physiques, perhaps to mirror fashion models.

This is an example of an excellent model who does not conform to the norm and is comfortable in herself. This pose lasted for over an hour; the author drew this sketch, his third attempt in about fifteen minutes. The model took fifteen minutes break to resume in a similar pose.

OVERHEARD IN A STUDIO

"Stand back from your work and tell me if the model's arms are longer than the legs." A long pause with no response from the student.

"Rob-Roy McGregor was said to have been able to tie/adjust his hose-garters without bending his back – such simian feats are rare."

Turning to the model: "Your surname is not McG, the forbidden name for Jacobites, is it?"

OVERHEARD IN A STUDIO

APOLLO'S BELT

In a discussion about the key characteristics of models in a Foundation course, one mature, female student told the very OAP male model during a break, that his distinctive curved feature was the curved bow below the abdominal muscles in the lower stomach.

"Thank you, that is known as *Adonis' belt*," he replied much flattered, for he was aware that his incipient 'pot-belliedness' was a trifle more pronounced than in his youth.

"Oh!" she said, "I did not know it had a name..."

On reflection in the middle of the next twenty minute pose, he realised that the term was probably *Apollo's girdle*. So he decided to look at a dictionary/encyclopoedia. He found:

Achilles was the son of a Greek god who was dipped in the Styx to give protection against mortal wounds. To retrieve him from the liquid he was held by the tendon on the back of his heel now known eponymously, Achilles tendon.

Apollyon was the greek Devil or destroyer.
Apollo was the god of agriculture; the son of Zeus.
Apollodoros was a Greek painter of BC408 who made great discoveries in perspective
Adonis was the lover of Aphrodite, the goddess of love.

There are butterflies named after both Adonis and Apollo, which presumably metamorphised from *pupae*.

Both Apollo and Adonis were the subject of many sculptures which are known on the 21st century – such as *Apollo Belvedere*. They are usually nude, sometimes fig-leaved and with the bodies of young boys, in which the bow-} of *amor* & archery are usually present.

They are the epitome – give-away diagnostic clue/key – to discriminate between what is acceptable as aesthetic in male nudes and conversely what is `verging on the obscene. This lead the group above into a discussion of what are the features which have been the accepted anthropometry of the ideal physique = the same for thousands of years?

It was suggested that it is the presence of several concavities such as the above girdle above, but also including the Achilles tendon of the heel, in fit unfat youth there are distinct areas where the skin is tight. In old age these disappear. Other concavities are the salt-cellar between the wrist and thumb where two tendons leave a bowl, which was favoured by 18th century snuff-taking men , who had observed that healthy, unfat, nubile young ladies showed this – while their other concavites were shrouded in garments.

A larger 'depression of the skin' is to be found above the clavicle (collar-bone).

The dimples at the base of the *dorsus longissimus*, where the skin covers bone.

Inter-costal muscles and ribs have distinctive cavities visible in fit men.

Lastly and by no means least, the arm-pits which when displayed in *diadumenos* poses rarely held for more than a mobile minute in real life, do display the charm of the curve inwards of the surface skin and outwards on the breasts and buttocks.

ALL the above are indicators of good health, youth and good diet. While if they are filled in by fat this may indicate insufficient exercise or an excess food intake- rendering the body less fit for breeding.

The convexities of the body are more obviously admired – biceps, bottoms/breasts, but not bellies. Aesthetics is the science of the philosophy of beauty which concerns art = poetry, music and the visual arts painting and sculpture: in that order. The one thing they have in common is the rhythm. The fluctuation of pentameter between long and short words and syllables, the silences and pauses between words and notes; the blank spaces on the paper between the convexities and concavities and of the bodies/ hills/buildings and vegetation

Other indicators in depictions of the male human form include a definite rhythm to the curvilinear contour of the legs, waist with a tapering of the limbs, indicating fine bone structure. Athletic strength vs. the brute force of the manual worker. The ratios of the lengths of bones should increase with a mathematical *phi* (that is the ratio of the sides of A2/3/4/5/ paper length to width). Look at the metacarpels = finger bones, they get longer towards the wrist in precisely that ratio. The foot is about the same length as the fore-arm = wrist to elbow. In most people there is some slight *displasia,* that is an inconsistency of these ratios, so that all the body parts do not have the same proportion, the legs may be very long but the body short, etc. In another dimension the face may not be symmetrical the right and left eyes may not be mirror images etc.. It is far from unusual for one leg [or other limb] to be longer than the other.

One final comment was made about unaesthetic male nudes. If the genitals were deemed enlarged whatever other attributes, they were not deemed aesthetic. Size, so it seems, matters perhaps inversely in a studio. Until the latter half of the 20th century, only classically proportioned penis and scrotum were depicted. Maybe because this is also healthy, indicating the shrinkage caused by swimming in cold water. Large flabby organs result from hot baths. Even the Greeks covered the pubic area of some gods' statues with a vine leaf – botanically very different from a fig but known as a fig leaf for some mysterious reason. Perhaps because it does not featured in fig.s 1-25.

Body Hair

It was common a generation ago for professional models to shave all their body hair. Nowadays male models need not shave more than normal, unless specifically asked to do so, and female models ought only shave as they normally do for their own cosmetic purposes. Hairy armpits and legs are after all very natural and so optional in 2005.

There were several reasons why shaving was fashionable/ obligatory.

Firstly, the indecency laws proscribed the exhibition of the private parts and the hair in those areas. Some laws stated that it was a crime to undress to the extent that pubic hair was visible. If the hair was shaved-off then the law was not being broken. This morality / legality custom was supposed to be applied both on stage and in art studios.

Secondly, hairs are sometimes a distraction; they confuse the outline and can even be ugly. They are better kept neat. However, some dark hairs, especially on an edge, can define a contour well by darkening its outline. Tutors are heard to say that there are no lines on the body edges. So hairs can be seen as either unhelpful or a useful adjunct. Much depends upon the light in which they are seen. Fine hairs can give a bloom to the skin. So beware of over-use of the razor.

Quicksand

In this composition, only the long-haired figure reclining might have been taken from a real pose. The illusion of his right arm being either missing or clutching an object which is out of view, perhaps his left hip, is as unresolved as the nature of the material between his right foot and the right elbow of the person whose right hip are closest to the viewer, and whose legs are under the reclining figure. The illusion of the [im]possibility of the scene is only apparent after scrutiny. The duration of the pose on dry land would depend on the strength of the left arm of the model - ten minutes unless the back is supported behind the long hair.

The apparent reality but actual [un]reality of the scene can be deduced by looking at the support for the main figure's right foot and at the left hip of the person gazing at him. The former's right elbow seems to be supporting the invisible foot. The whole body weight is supported by the left arm. This is an example of how not to overdo the twist. Also, the reclining figure is either one-armed or his right hand is hidden by his long hair.

The group pose depicted is imaginary - made up from many sketches and memory.

BREATHING

Models need to understand about the basics of breathing as it will help them minimise unavoidable movement. The lungs can be ventilated in two ways: a) the ribs and chest can be expanded and contracted; and b) the diaphragm and stomach can be used to push up and down under the lungs. Both are normally within voluntary control. The danger of holding one's breath or trying to breathe with very short, soft puffs are obvious. Heavy breathing causes the human body to hyperventilate which increases the amount of carbon dioxide blown out of the system and disturbs the body acid balance. Some people pant without realising it, especially when they are under stress. So models should think about their rate of breathing from time to time and vary it deliberately. Normal breathing is abdominal; hyperventilation and deep breathing involve the ribs.

Changes in carbon-dioxide account for some 'meditation' states. Models may feel that going into a trance is one way of passing the time, the writer prefers some mental exercises such as checking on breathing, repeating memorised poetry or other mind games.

Another physiological effect experienced by male models perhaps associated with changes in breathing patterns is a secretion from the Cowper's gland. This is the clear fluid which flows from the penis as a lubricant. It is not controllable but is thought by medical specialists to rely on some psychological stimulus. Not all men are aware that it has occurred. It ought not to cause embarrassment, being more or less an acceptable bodily function. Usually someone who has noticed it will suggest that it is time for the model to take a break. Thus at the risk of a bad pun on breathing, it is a good rule for models to plan the timing of their 'pantlessness' if they suspect a flow from Cowper's or any other gland.

BALANCE

Both the physiology and psychology of keeping one's balance as a model deserve some attention; for all models must be well balanced mentally, and to remain in a good pose, they must also have full control over their own physical, mental balance.

The **gravity** of the job can maybe a trifle over-simplified if used as the prime job description as to what to look for in potential models, but it does describe much of what is needed.

In physical terms the centre of gravity of any stable object must be within the triangle of three static points, each of which can be drawn as vertical lines. The further apart these points are, the more stable the object will be in 'statics & dynamic' conditions. The exact position of centres of gravity of each person varies. Generally it is between the navel and lower sternum; more or less inside the centre of the belly. Its position moves as limbs and head are moved. It is only possible to somersault by exploiting these changes. Models need to be aware of where their C of G [centre of gravity] is in each pose.

The sense organ that tells us about changes in the centre of gravity is a 'spirit level' near the ears. The three points are the heels and toes of two feet. As we walk, one of the four is redundant. As humans get older they get less accurate input from the nerves in their feet; this is why some older models often have difficulty in standing poses. So some add stability by using a broom-handle/pole/or thumb-stick as a third static point, the other two being the feet. These supports can also be used to keep an arm in the air at a definite level, for even after a minute pose an unsupported limb of Hercules himself can sag.

Sight-lines and mirrors can help the model to watch any change of position.

ROYAL ACADEMY 'LESSONS FOR LIFE'

In 1994, the Royal Academy for Arts and the Midland Bank mounted a programme to encourage the study of life in schools in England. It was called 'Outreach for Secondary Schools'. An excellent booklet of 46 pages was published (ISBN 0- 900946 43 1). It traces **life** teaching in London from 1768 and shows students drawing from statues in the Antique School of New Somerset House to the pilot project in 1988 using Henry Moore's sculptures from the RA in an Outreach programme.

The booklet deals with the history of the attitudes of civil servants in Ministries of Education to the use of nude *vs* clothed models. The last half describes some reactions of students and teachers and shows their work and the groups working.

The final couple of pages gives the reactions of the models. These were photographed while working in gymnasia rather than studios. 'Gym' aptly means nude. The students used the floor rather than easels and desks. The role of the model in educating the students was emphasised. Many of the students had not realised the models were themselves artists. Indeed, one admitted to imagining the model was mindless – unable to think, at the start of the day. By evening, the scales had dropped. Also that if he had known the model was not a statue, the process of starting to draw would have been much more difficult.

There was also a deliberate attempt to avoid any formal life studio ambience. Both models and tutors included words and poetry in their role – surprisingly, there was no mention of music; one deduces there was none.

GROUP DYNAMICS

Students of psychology and sociology, in which the dynamic interrelationships between members of any group is of core interest , will recognise the unusual features of a life class. For the focal figure is mainly silent, static and has disrobed while all the others are clad and chatter only in short breaks at intervals.

In most groups of six or more there are roles such as leader, jester-cum-joker, moral censor, deputy leader in waiting. The way in which these are assumed depends on many factors; for example the leadership role is usually assumed by tacit tests of competitors' power-base/popularity – assertiveness.

In any teaching situation the teacher is automatically given the place/honour of being the *ex officio* accepted leader. In other life class groups the organiser who booked the model is usually the accepted leader. The duty of announcing the duration of poses and ensuring the model is allowed to rest and relax appropriately is often delegated by the leader or assumed by another – in other circumstances these are the role of the moral conscience of the group. The jester role emerges when someone feels a need to reduce tension when there is any incipient conflict or confrontation.

In life classes the centre of attention is obviously the model, however as uniquely no eye contact nor any verbal or body language is observable, the model is not perceived as a full member of the group. Herein is a source of the sense of being an 'outsider'. It is the duty of the leader of the group to stress frequently that the ***most important person in the studio*** is the model *sine qua non* – (without which NOTHING).

Each member of the group should make an individual effort to recognise the model as being the central member of the group. The joker will usually make light comments about the poses to ease any tensions. Late-comers present a problem for the roles already adopted at the start may need to be changed as a dominant late-comer may be well-known. That alone is sometimes a good reason for closing the doors once a session has started.

In one group where there were some twenty members of whom half attended randomly for morning sessions, the models had observed that the group dynamics were often very complex. There were several alternative leaders, etc. The choice of pose would take up to 15% of the time. Arguments, slight changes on lighting and refusal to move from the territory of a preferred and habitual place in the studio. This delay was to the model's benefit for poses were interspersed by long periods of debate within the group.

It is important for those organising life classes to recognise the group dynamic interactions and to set the scene, by having a well accepted code of conduct – silence, absolute silence, music, polite introductions of the model if new to the group, announcing durations clearly and having one person responsible for setting the pose with the approval of the model.

In one four-day residential life tutorial aimed at liberating energies, some fifteen students and three nubile young models, two girls and a man, ended with the students being invited to emulate the models. They had become accustomed to the use of quick poses, music and rhythm unusual use of left and right hands with sticks and feathers to make large marks. Throughout the previous three days the professional models had danced alone, in couples or even as a threesome – nude. After the first two students, ladies, had posed an OAP male asked permission to strip off – at the end of the five minutes he was applauded and followed nude by most of the rest of the group, who were told it was their choice. The group dynamic and satisfaction was that the division between the free, joyous, expression of their own feelings which the models had demonstrated was shared and the group felt they too had joined them in a single group. Spontaneously.

Starting a Group

The experience of groups is that not all members are able to attend all or even half of the meetings. So the first step is to find a room for hire where there is an 'elastic' possibility of few = 7 – many = ca.20 spaces. But space for half the membership (40 in the example) is usually excessive. The room should have some chairs. If members do not possess their own easels then two chairs <u>each</u> are needed; one for a seat, the other to rest the drawing board on.

A half day or even just two and a half hours per week will suffice for a start.

Models can usually be found via the local art college or from notices or messages in local art suppliers. RAM, mentioned herein, is another source.

If the room has a store then a mattress or mats and a chair or other 'props' such as a mirror can be kept there. A supply of drapes and background screens also help – particularly if chequered for easy measurement. The person organising will also need to arrange suitable heating- an electric fan/heater and some lights. It can be a tiresome chore to arrive with all these and then find the model has not turned up. That is when a career as an artist/model often starts. But if no one is prepared to step into Prynne's footprints or sandals (she was ever bare footed) then the group will have to be content with portraits. Twenty minutes per person is normal.

The person who books the model should also have **sole responsibility** for setting the pose and its duration with the agreement of the model. This is the reward for all the time spent on the phone, etc. The comfort of the model should by contrast be **everyone's duty**. The occasional word – "OK for heat?" or "Do you need a break yet?" – is far better than absolute silence. New models can often be coaxed into interesting poses by being asked to catch a soft ball or cushion thrown by the organiser. They can also be told about sight-lines and suitable objects found for them to use.

One member (preferably the heaviest fit male) of the group should be assigned the duty of keeping the entry door shut and uninvited visitors at bay. Another keen regular member can bring the music.

LIBERATED LIFE CLASSES

In London in the late 1990's, a Mme Dupres, a French artist, had the idea of a unisex art group. This was successful and for a time attracted attention on the women's lib scene. However it ignored some basic facts of life and life drawing. The universal animal kingdom is made up of two genders and life drawing is usually asexual in the clinical way in which the model is supposedly observed.

The main concern of Ladies Only, Liberated Life Drawing Classes is the welfare of the model, who works with, rather than for, the group. For to be naked outside one's own domestic setting, especially when surrounded by clothed strangers is a rather 'surreal' situation. It can be a vulnerable, if not threatening, one. In liberated life drawing, every effort is made to solve some of the model's problems, lack of comfort, isolation, absence of communication between 'artist' and 'model', boredom and exposure to hazard. By contrast in other life classes the modernist approach to the female figure can reduce it to an empty vessel, with beautiful forms, simplified, de-contextualised, fragmented and reduced to the equivalent of a bowl of fruit or a landscape.

SOME THOUGHTS ON 'NATURISM'

Naturism is a long word used to make *nudism* sound more sophisticated, and so more normal and less naked.

Whereas in English-speaking parts of the world, the majority are assumed to be against people swimming or sun-bathing publicly in the nude, elsewhere there are less inhibiting attitudes. In darkest Africa where once the naked savage roamed unadorned and unashamed, now the zealots of religions have deemed that state uncivilised and made them wear bras and pants as a minimum. Sad and not as sanitary or hygienic.

It might be assumed that all models are also nudists. Not so. But the same holds for the reverse assumption for many, indeed most, nudists shrink at the idea of being a life model. However, models generally have sympathy with naturists and wish that there were more places where swimming and sun-bathing was legal in public. Naturists must find private places, known as colonies, for some reason, if they are to avoid intrusive exhibitionists. The nudist beach at Brighton and the Sandbanks area near Poole Harbour are both notorious for such. Even the National Trust is unable to get people to behave with natural decency and consideration for others. Again, a sad reflection on our mores.

Legislators internationally seem to have wildly different standards. In Germany, FKK (Frei Korpur Kultur) is displayed on signs where, if people so wish, they can discard swimwear – or not. The same code applies in former Jugoslavia. In Munich, the lake in a central park deems costume optional. It is said that those who swim the lake length then board buses to return without a stitch or a pocket for the fare. Anglophones are less tolerant and less open-minded.

It would seem only fair that if, say, 10% of the UK population want to bathe without costume that 10% of the beaches and parks should have areas designated for them where they will not offend those whose still think sight of their bodies can damage their chances of salvation, or have similar un-natural phobias. If only 5% or some other % then *pro rata*.

The German attitude towards bodies was altered during the 3rd Reich. The Food Magazine quoted G...H..'s 'History of the 3rd Reich' as evidence that the Nazis had a cult of body beautiful and Aryan perfection, in which the body became a part-owned by the state, separated from the self. Prior to that the self and body were seen as indivisible. Women became breeding machines while men were the perfect, fit, sculpted wonders. The wonder nation.

MUSHROOMS GROW WILD

Here is a story about three young men who when they were asked to model for art classes decided after audition that, as they had been sun bathing with trunks [swimwear], that they would look much better if they attained an even all-over tan. For they were lily white where their boxers/Y fronts had shaded the middle bits; they knew that even tiny bikini lines can distract artists .

So they visited a local naturist beach where they disported themselves in the sand-dunes. They soon realised that the best results would come if they covered up all those parts already golden. So they covered themselves with sand – top and bottom. Neither trunks nor legs were visible. Only the middle bits became irradiated.

They fell asleep, at midday, when three little old ladies strayed onto the site, on a nature walk.

"Oh! Goodness me!" one cried, "whatever can those things be?"

"They are certainly not snakes," said the herpetologist.

"Nor are they mushrooms," cried the youngest, a mycologist [fungi expert].

The third pondered and then said, in a very thin voice: "I know what those things are. When I was a young gal, my mother told me all about the birds and bees and then sent me around the world on a cruise to find one." After a gasp of breath, she shouted: **"Isn't this marvelous – to find three, and all growing wild…"**

STREAKERS COMPARED WITH LIFE MODELS

Streaking is a relatively new phenomenon; a person who in a crowded public venue suddenly strips off then runs through the crowd or into the public eye often at a games pitch, or protester site.

At first sight, the speed and lack of acquiescence by the crowd/audience make the actions different from that of modelling. The offender – who may have offended the prudish whose feelings ought to be respected – is often apprehended by the police and the naughty bits covered by a helmet or other headgear. This causes much amusement and laughter; we find anything which draws attention to illogical taboos mirthful.

Streakers do however often have an intention to shock and draw attention to themselves; whether they recognise this or not is a matter for psychologists.

Some models become so accustomed to being nude in public that they too ponder streaking as a means of drawing attention to the laws and customs which while protecting the prudish from sights they might find offensive, deny freedom to those who may wish to feel the joy of being nude amongst the clothed whenever they wish to be cool – in both senses of that word.

While pondering the above readers may find helpful an anecdote about the Old Folks Home in which some elderly persons decided to streak (with the intention of getting the attention of others of the opposite gender): it may help illuminate the fact that we get more tolerant with age.

As the bevy passed those sitting in a row of chairs one person said to neighbours: "Do you know what that was?"

"I seem to remember I saw one just like it – a very long time ago," said the right-side

The left side replied: "I don't remember what it's called either."

At which the right hand interrupted with: "But whatever it was, it needed ironing!"

Age and wrinkles are not at all unacceptable in life models – indeed they are welcomed as they present a new challenge, if un-ironed.

By contrast to streakers, there is a new phenomenon of group nudity as in Stephen Tunnick's photo of the 'Cutty Sark' organised by David Bowie for photographs. In this the waves were made of hundreds of naked bodies (which are 80+% water) – but each wave is recognisably human. It is a splendid image.

OVERHEARD IN A STUDIO

Heard by a lady model about a male model
"Did you hear that Eric the model is going to retire?"
"Who's Eric?"
"You know, he is the one who is said to be a flasher on his day-off…"
"Well, they say he is going to *stick-it-out* for another year."

REST

Ergonomists a few decades ago tried to establish that the stress of work in all occupations could be by measured by heart-beat, but this was later proved not to be the sole criterion. The general principle is that the greater the change in heart-beat the greater the need for rest and pay to compensate for the effort. The work of models was used to demonstrate that other factors must be taken into consideration when pay and rest are to be treated fairly and scientifically. In the debate between work scientists in letters to their learned journals, the example of the stress of an art model was used to de-bunk the 'heartbeat alone' theory. For an artist drawing a nubile model might have a much higher heart rate but could not be said to be doing more work than the stationary model. The *reductio ad absurdum* technique of exposing the absurdity of the theory worked – as it is hoped the exposure of the taxmens' antics will also reintroduce sanity to the system.

REST BREAKS

All workers need rest, even if they are not moving. Modelling is a classic example of a job in which no mental or physical work is, at first sight, being done: yet where there is a real need for relaxation and recovery from a very fatiguing and demanding task.

There is an International Labour Office, ILO, convention to which all United Nations countries subscribed. Their REST allowances for all manner of work have been agreed by both Trades Unions and employers, who accept the basic science on which these are based. Sadly few artists or tutors seem to have heard of them. Tables showing how much rest is needed are published

155

in books on ergonomics and work science, such as the ILO's "Introduction to Work Study" published in 1962 in Geneva. It is a near classic, in umpteen editions, in many languages. Its tables for allowances have international acceptance by management scientists who have studied the medical and ergonomic problems of productivity.

To maximise productivity the slave drivers' approach is useless. Wise managers and keen workers, particularly the self-employed, know that more can be achieved if rest is taken appropriately. They know that a change is as good as a rest. Models cannot change their pose. They do need extra paid time for changing their garb and recovering from the strain of posing. Keeping a model non-stop on the podium until the bell rings for the end of a session robs the model; unless extra time is paid for.

The FREQUENCY of taking rest and the RATIO of time worked to that needed to recover from its effects must be considered separately. The total percentage of rest for models will range from fifteen percent (the absolute minimum) to over fifty percent, a not uncommon proportion. That is posing for only forty minutes per paid hour. Posing should be for only ten minutes in very strenuous positions: even sitting poses need some rest after half an hour.

Sessions often begin with four to six warm-up poses of, say, five minutes each. Although only a minute pause is taken between each, the cumulative rest needed and earned may be over ten minutes. This might be added to the tea-break after two longer poses of half and hour each. These attract a further minimum often minutes: making a total of twenty minutes due for payment.

New models will feel the need to relax much more than experienced models, but both earn the right to be reimbursed for their effort expended.

Suggested rates should be-
Dress and undress: 10 minutes = 20 per session.**
Basic needs, e.g. toilet and refreshments, (coffee), etc.: 6% of time worked.
Sitting and prone poses: 8-12% of time worked taken hourly or at lesser intervals

Thus for a two hour session 20 mins plus 16 mins (6% + say 10% of 2 hours less 20 = 100) = 36 minutes

Standing poses: 15 to 20% taken half hourly
Action poses: 25+% taken before limbs begin to shake.

The total for a strenuous session of 2 hours would be a further 15 minutes added to the example, above making 41 minutes to be paid for.

It is dangerous to allow limbs to become numbed or lose circulation. Movement prevents lactic acid accumulation. It is sadly not rare for models to faint; all present in a studio who are looking at the model have a duty to speak to the model before this happens. The prime cause is insufficient rest breaks for the model some of whom feel a duty to struggle on against their natural warnings system.

In many cases of short sessions the model may choose not to take the rest earned on site but to recuperate after the session. It is not acceptable for them to be expected to work every minute of the hours paid for (at a basic minimum wage or even £10 per hour) without extra pay for the extra rest earned.

If the contract is for an eight hour day on the podium there would be an additional 40 minutes changing time. The basic 6% of 480 mins worked amounts to:

two 15 minute tea breaks. In addition, depending on the nature of the poses, assuming 15% average, a further HOUR+ is due. All of this might not be taken in the studio; for the artists may be keen to resume work before the full rest has been taken.

** The exact duration will depend on the location of the studio to the toilets and changing area. Also the delays in getting forms signed for payment and other official bureaucracy.

PAY AND TAX

The rates of pay internationally vary widely; here are a few examples:

Pre-war: a franc a day in Paris – tax free.

1980: $4 per hour in Canada, often tax free.

For 2005: £10 +/- per hour in London; £8 elsewhere in UK

€15 per hour in France – more in Paris

all before tax.

US$40 per hour for the best models in Mexico

but only $2 for average regular models.

Post-war: in 1950 Tam (Sean) Connery earned 7/0d an hour. This is 1/20th of the 2005 rate.

The major problem in the UK is the inappropriate interest of taxmen in artistic miniscule incomes. Vast quantities of paper are used for very small sums of money. This is a major factor in preventing more people offering their services as occasional models. Intrusive inquisitiveness by tax man and personnel administrators is uncalled for in what is basically self-employment.

RAM* has set target fees per hour worked, based on London. But internationally, the rates per hour for a full day, half day and a two-hour session should also reflect the costs of travel and the time needed to get to the studio. Some suggested rates are given below.

* RAM = Register of Artists' Models, www.modelreg.com

SUGGESTED RATES

Additional fees based on the agreed minimum rate, that is the RAM rate of the basic minimum wage plus 75% for:

ENERGETIC POSES – 25% increase on hourly rate

SHORT SESSIONS – any session of under four hours, extra hour travelling time.

The general rule *for drawing* seems to be the less worn, the less earned. The shorter the session, the lower the rewards. But for <u>photos</u> the reverse holds. For while some models can earn great riches – fashion and photographic models, for example – life models have, from time immemorial, been paid very little for their time. Photographic models are paid in some art colleges four times the life models' fee. Yet the former are paid for a few seconds exposure after many hours of preparation. It is their loss of anonymity though exposure in the other (non-photographic) sense of the word that is the main factor.

Pay for most jobs is usually based on hours worked. These must by law include time for rest and preparation. As standing poses are much harder work than prone or sitting poses, in fairness the rates of pay should relate to the onerous nature of the job. Some tutors do not even seem to be aware of the need for rest in arduous poses. Those administrators who try to make job evaluation comparisons have failed to understand how difficult it is to remain still for long periods. Another important consideration is supply and demand; there is a pool of unemployed talent by comparison with the hours of work available and the cash to pay for it. Any scarcity of talent results in an increase in pay rates.

<u>**As one of the purposes of this book is to encourage more private groups to share the costs of hiring models, it is hereby emphasised that they should reward the models less niggardly than those who use taxpayers' funds for adult education. A fee of £4 for a two-hour session per artist is enough if more than six share, to meet the basic RAM rate of £10 in UK. Ten artists could pay more.**</u> In many cities there are groups where 15-20 meet regularly. So £12 per hour plus travel is reasonable and fair. But the total earnings compared to the pay per hour is important. £10 per hour is unacceptable unless at least three hours are paid for.

Travel time and cost is ignored by all except the most enlightened studios.

Having regard to the fact that taxpayers' money is used for most models' salaries, it is fair to expose the great injustice of the Income Tax Department in UK when dealing with part-time casual workers. It is high time that the tax officials reviewed their **most unfair** ruling that travel and expenses cannot be deducted before tax for all part-time peripatetic employees, working on many sites far from home. These Treasury rules are foolish and deserve political scrutiny. While clothing allowances are inappropriate for nude models, many life models provide costumes without any hire charge. Tax deductions for costume, travel and for expenses, phones ought to be deductible as most bookings are made at short notice by phone. That income tax gathering costs far exceed any tax levied is obvious.

The problem of pay can only be solved if both employers and the taxmen collaborate. The current deluge of form-filling appears to cost the government as much as the fees earned, in ridiculous clerical effort. This burden falls on government, local employers and employees. A model working for a few hours for each of several employers is expected to fill in income tax forms in the UK for each employer. Some state employers do not pay a cheque until the end of the month following the work done. Small wonder some potential models decline to work unless they are paid over £8 per hour for a minimum of four hours.

Once-upon-a-time, tutors paid in cash. Since then, bureaucracy has run riot and destroyed the simplicity of a system which provided part-time relief and much leisure pleasure. With little or no net benefit to the government.

In private studios where a group pool the costs for two hours per week, the cost is £4 per session. From a local authority adult education programme, the cost is £34 for ten two hour sessions. The former had a max of six artists the latter ten; they also had a tutor at £15 per hour.

The tax collected and returned is similarly daft. Most models pay no tax.

The average artist in UK earned under £5,000 in 2004. Many worldwide also work as artist models to earn an extra crust.

GUIDELINES

MODELS

1.Get a repeat of the date time and venue from whoever made the booking, written and verbal if possible

2. Bring a robe, slippers and towel

3. Avoid direct eye contact while posing

4. Set several sight-lines

5. Give ample warning if the pose is to be ended before the agreed time set

6. Avoid being either too shy and silent or too voluble

7. Bring your own heater / bits of carpet for warmth

8. Bring your own props: broomstick, rope, balloon

ARTIST - STUDENTS

1. Leave an ample gangway for the model to enter and exit to the changing area

2. Do not stare as the model disrobes

3. Always thank the model and if a 'first' applaud / clap at the end of the session.

4. Avoid direct eye contact

5. Do not move any object the model may be using as a part of the sight-lines

6. Avoid giving the impression that you think models are lesser mortals or less attractive than you might like.

STUDIO ORGANISERS

1. Provide the model on arrival with details of pose lengths, pay, location of toilets / mirrors / changing areas (with coat hangers and chair)

2. Introduce the model using their nom-de-pose

3. Mark each pose long before the time-limit (which should be set before it starts and repeated)

4. Check with the model frequently to ensure that the pose is not becoming arduous or impossible to hold.

5. After each break or rest-period check with the group to ensure the position is the same as before and if any dispute this check that they are in exactly (as is humanly possible) the same position as before – most often it is the student (not the model) who moved!

6. Make the cash collection or pay slip form well beforehand. If paying by the hour time for changing and collecting pay must be paid for

7. Do not try to get the model to take up poses which are too twisted to hold for long. If extending the duration of a pose always ask the model first if this is possible

8. With new models for action poses have a cushion or tennis ball to throw to be caught and held

9. Have plenty of props – balloons, mats, stools, ropes (with ceiling hooks), chairs,

10. Have a studio clock and also call out the time – an egg timer which 'pings' helps with short poses.

11. Make sure that all present understand that the MOST important person in the studio is the model (SINE QUA NON) that is because without the model there is no life-class

OVERHEARD IN A STUDIO

The 'cadging nephew', was the reason an elderly model gave for earning a few quid in his dotage and retirement, by modelling at the local art college. It was so that he could tell those who sought to borrow a 'fiver' from him that they could have as easily earned it as he had. There are many on the dole or otherwise 'unwaged' who, if they had the moral fibre and less silly inhibitions, could add to the variety of models available locally.

AUDIT AND AUDITION

An **audit** is the process of third parties checking on suitability and accuracy.

An **audition** is an interview in which a particular individual's suitability for an acting or singing part or job is assessed.

The process of auditioning models can be summarised as the 'mantle falling-off' one pair of shoulders onto another – generation after generation – as we suggest in our dedication. Just as the employer must be sure the model is well suited so the employee needs assurances that the venue is of acceptable standards. So studio audits are offered by the authors and others. The third check on the three parties – studio, model, artists – is assurances that the artists are genuine and not voyeurs and so on. Personal recommendations are more usual between open studios where artists and models and artist-models network.

A job interview and initial training with an outline of the job requirements and local customs and standards is usual for most employment. 'Sitting alongside Nellie' to learn the job – Nellie being an experienced worker – was usual in many occupations. Sadly, many models are expected to start work without any explanations or guidance.

It has recently become usual, and even necessary, for new models to be auditioned before they are employed or recommended for work. This is especially true where membership of organisations such as the Register of Artists' Models (RAM) is concerned. **Auditions** may be combined with their open studio sessions, as they provide schools and studios with models, some of whom may be unknown to either party/ individual. It is a different matter where an artist seeks models for a solo studio. There the approach is usually made by the artist to anyone who they perceive as a potential portrait/ figure. Some artists are well known for approaching pulchritudinous persons with the chat-up line:

"I wonder if you would pose for me? I am a genuine artist", no audition needed.

Colleges may engage a potential model for a short 'trial sitting', which is in essence an audition. If the person fidgets or cannot hold the pose then they are not employed again. One lady at the Royal College of Art was so coy, clutching her gown, that to make her more comfortable, the tutor asked her to pose prone under a sheet all day. She liked this so much that she asked to come again – sadly missing the point that a model must be seen 100% nude.

An **audit** of the studio facilities by models may be a useful reverse inspection. For from the models' point of view, many studios are deficient in basic features. The check list in the guide lines and the criticisms of changing areas are mentioned elsewhere on these pages. Attitudes towards the timing of rest-breaks can be discussed and agreed in a studio audit. The days when a tutor omnipotently decreed the terms for the model are past.

Before describing the audition procedure for a model agency such as RAM, perhaps an examination of the attitudes behind the term may help in understanding the minds of the parties involved. For it can also be a cover for introducing all parties to the protocol expected .

To 'audition' for a job that involves absolute silence may seem to be oxymoronic (a contradiction in terms). The job specification is to remain absolutely[1] nude, silent and motionless. But what word other than audition describes the process by which persons desiring employment as models can be ' vetted '. That word also suggests that the bodies are animal; or lacking in humanity. Continuing in this vein, to suggest that the process is quasi-medical- doctoring would be even worse. In an effort to create an ambience of squeaky cleanliness in studios, in the

---

[1] 'Absolutely' is the author's pet hate word – absolute zero is the absence of heat, beyond which nature cannot go; in common parlance it has become a superlative, which it is not.

moral sense[2] de-eroticising has become a cult. To this end, the role of model must be choreographed – before, during and after the actual pose.

The first step of an audition is for the auditor, after normal civilities, to ask the applicant **in the presence of another person** to "please get undressed" and then show them the screen or changing area from which to emerge . The potential model should then be left alone. Robes were usually provided if deemed necessary, for the entry from the dressing room to podium until quite recently. But by 2001, this was no longer seen as obligatory. Robes are optional and the applicant should be left to decided on this point themselves, bringing their own. The interviewer and chaperone should then ask for a few short poses to draw. This avoids the indignity of anatomical scrutiny and staring eyes.

Ideally the auditioning studio is a part of a larger studio, in which work is in progress or during a rest period/tea-break. The open studio used by RAM was in an alcove off a much larger studio in which two models were posing for an open studio of some 30 artists. A muscular man with splendid dreadlocks and beard with a nubian nubile lady, of near Naomi Campbell physique, both were black-skinned, posed on adjacent plinths. This allowed the new model to see how a studio works. In the main studio the pair alternated between short poses of ten minutes and longer seated poses of forth-five minutes.

At the far end of the hall was the auditioning alcove studio where a young man who had occasionally modelled before was to be tried out. He was clearly slightly apprehensive; lacking in experience and self- assurance. When asked to pose for ten minutes he took up a standing pose with his left arm well over his head. This was too ambitious and soon his arm moved – ten, then twenty, degrees while his head also sank. His second pose when crouching in a difficult 'knot' was much better and difficult to draw. He knew what poses would be useful but not how to hold them. The RAM official gave him some hints and he progressed to longer poses.

[2] They are often unspeakably dirty in terms of domestic hygiene and need an AUDIT.

The advantage of the arrangement was that a new model was not the sole focus of attention, for the artists had the opportunity and unusual luxury to draw on variety. Auditions can be replaced by letting new models pose in groups with others – but this is expensive and only possible for studios with numerous clientele.

One aspect of audio (being heard) is the focus of a very common phobia to which even very experienced models will confess. The audible effect is too delicate to express in print without a preamble.

Biologically every body is a tube to digest food with which to support the energy requirements of the four limbed vehicle which supports the brain. A rhyming couplet may help:

> *"I am a tube, which eats food that's been chewed -*
> *the other end is considered rude."*

In reverse order of (c)rudity, the biological process ends with gas, liquid and solids.

Tummy rumblings are involuntary and can occur without warning, so models beware of a meal of 'noisy oysters' before working. If strange noises are heard in the silence, the best thing is to blame someone else – and if denials brand him as not being a gentleman. Music and talking help to make the atmosphere comfortable / agreeable.

The model's worst fear is an incontrollable fart. This is often preceded by a bloated abdomen. The next symptom, in studios where the model is NOT encouraged to take rest pauses as and when they wish, is clenched buttock muscles and then teeth.

The preceding should be read in the context of items **not** overheard in a studio.

PREGNANCY

The authors know of at least five ladies who have continued modelling for regular sessions well into pregnancies. This may surprise some but the natural form and healthy condition as the changes occurred were a joy shared by many including both parents and the childless.

It may be significant that two were single mums, determined to provide a good life for their child which they managed in exemplary fashion. Three were teachers in schools for very young children.

Obviously care is needed to ensure that poses do not put any awkward strain on such models. It is not a bad idea for groups to treat all ladies as if they might be pregnant.

OVERHEARD IN A STUDIO

Moth Inspectorate

Insects can be a pest to models In the Dordogne, the A*telier Mouche* is named on account of the hoards of flies and so on, which seem attracted more to the model than to the others, who are more free to slap. Most models can aim a well targeted slap at an itch or fly while remaining corseted in the pose.

The following tale may help new models who anticipate situations in which they may have to explain an absence of their attire.

A male model was invited to the home of a lady artist; it soon became clear to him that her ideas/plans extended beyond artistic endeavours. For – after he had already disrobed – she suddenly undressed and invited him upstairs.

Unexpectedly her husband returned and called out:

"Darling – I'm home, where are you?"

"Quick," she said to the model, "into the bathroom."

"I'm in the bedroom," she shouted. "Just a minute and I will be down."

"Don't bother, I am already on the stairs."

The husband, meeting her halfway and supposing she was eagerly awaiting his attentions: "So! I'll just pop into the bathroom, to get ready."

As he closed the door he spotted a stranger. "What are you doing in my bathroom, SIR!"

"Oh! Quite simple," said he, most calmly. "This place is infested; it is the very worst case I have ever been to." The quick-thinking model clapped his hands upon imaginary insects and slapped the husband on the face and back as he spied yet another offending (but invisible) beast. "Thousands of them – **clothes moths** – all over the place. Look! They have already eaten ALL my clothes. I am from the *Insect Inspectorate* – you are very lucky I got here in time "

With another slap on his neck, he sprayed the husband in the face with a handy can of the hair-setting varnish used by ye artist-wife to fix charcoal and pastel, and fled the scene.

Models called on to enact body-language poses can use the situations described above as a source of inspiration. Charades and Mime.

Heraldry

Heraldic poses are included because they are usually the exact opposite of what is needed for artistic purposes. The other reason is that they use an arcane terminology which is precise, allowing only one interpretation of the written code. As with the names of body parts. Arms* are confrontational; there is military precision, clarion import. The human hand is depicted in palm-up view with all fingers equally spaced and equidistant. Such is rarely viewed in life or a studio. But the hand is most easily recognised from this view, as a badge of baronets.

In Scottish heraldry, there are examples of the nude human form for which presumably a life model posed. These illustrate an olde worlde attitude to public nudity. On a full scale shield the form will be a quarter life sized.

The main use of nude figures is as supporters, that is those who hold the shield upright, as an indication of nobility; often genders are mixed, gents dexter/right; ladies sinister/left. Often described as savage, meaning nude and unshaven! Supporters usually 'stand at ease'; that is in a pose which is more restful than 'at attention'.

The human form is used as a charge (the main theme); crescents, mullets, sheaves of wheat and all manner of shapes are more common

---

* Arms as in coats of – not the shoulder to hand body part – are described in an arcane code. Proper means "as in nature", see p.193.

az = azure = blue
or = gold
arg = argent – silver

175

The Dalzell or Dalzeil family once Earls of Carnwath[1] "carried a man" on their arms.

While the Sandemans[2] of port-wine fame, have a woman. Note the refinement of designations as either lady or gent OR male and female are eschewed. Technically, gentlemen are those having coats of arms, yeoman do not.

The backgrounds are also of interest as backdrops. The man is against a sable fur of jet matt black while the woman is cast in golden rays of sun light against silver [argent]. The man might be expected to be well tanned while the woman might be untanned, framed in a blue gold star spangled border. Aesthetically, the backdrops might have been better if reversed – but heralds clearly knew best.

The exact detail of the poses is not specified with sufficient detail to prescribe some imaginative gestures – nor is the colour of the book – while a full frontal view is given there seems to be no real reason why a side of even back-view would be any less correct. The word 'proper' is an heraldic term meaning 'as in nature'.

Coats of arms are, like the human form, symmetrical about a central axis, spine = pale. They can only be depicted from eye level at their centre with the shield at right angles to the plane of vantage. Thus requiring no perspective, it is the use of a knowledge of perspective which is demanding in life drawing; for although the right arm is usually the same length as the left, it will never appear so in a drawing, unless the pose is for Dalzell above or a frog ready for dissection.

Drawing tricks (sketches) of arms is an exercise akin to life drawing. It demands a sense of balance and hand-eye coordination. Heraldic art is a sadly neglected area of creativity no longer fashionable but requiring great skill and precision absent in so much of what today passes as art.

[1] Sable: a naked man with arms extended proper. Crest: A dagger erect proper.
Motto 'I DARE'
[2] Argent: a naked woman standing on a globe, issuing from the base, in her dexter (right) hand a book and in her sinister (left) a palm branch: upon her breast the sun in spleandour and flowing round her figure a web of linen proper: all within a bordure az. (blue) charged with 8 mullets or (gold).

Nudity, Vanity, Physiques And Prudery

The British and other Anglophone attitudes towards nudity were always reserved. Robert Browning wrote a poem ridiculing a lady who regarded nude modelling as amoral yet she wore dead birds on her hat. For him nude modelling was not amoral while killing birds was totally immoral.

Oscar Wilde wrote a book about Dorian Gray, a male model. He remained young and beautiful externally while corrupt within. Why was he so, what was his self image?

A group of models met to discuss the need to recruit new models to pose in the nude. They commenced the session by thinking about why it was that they were deemed to be slightly insane just because they were prepared to take-off their clothes in public.

One person suggested that most models wanted to prove that their bodies were desirable; this was probably a result of past rejection. Another then became more confessional and admitted that he was also interested in naturism and had joined a club with luxurious premises, but as a single man he had not been very welcome. As that had not been successful he now went for long moonlit walks in the nude in forests – even national parks.

Another then chimed in with a list of open water areas in which he had swum without clothes. His work had taken him to tropical shores where the sands of the Indian Ocean had started his compulsion to collect places on a global coastal map. He even went to Canada where the icy lakes of the Rockies in spring are a particular challenge, especially getting to a block of ice when the shore-line was thawed and the water was just above freezing-point. He had also swum naked in seas and oceans around the world.

His eclectic list of bathing places included Goa and the opposite side of the Indian Ocean, the Isles of Scilly, the sandbanks off Bournemouth, and the west of France.

One model, a former soldier, had moved on to 'strippagram' work, which paid very well, after he had become accustomed to being nude on parade. Others enjoyed the naked state by taking walks or bicycle rides on country roads when the moon was high and full.

Being photographed in the nude is now thought [see Observer Magazine 6 February 2005] to be therapeutic in improving the body satisfaction of some women – anorexics and bulimia sufferers, etc. In a less dramatic way, life modelling as in 'Calendar Girls' is an important step towards self-awareness.

Many models are former art students who started modelling when there was a last minute need for a replacement. Some of course turn to nude modelling solely for the money it offers but this seemed to be the exception rather than the rule. Overall it seems that most models enjoy the state of nakedness itself and often take the time to seek solitary, silent circumstances where they can express the freedom which it grants, without the need for company.

The career of nude modelling is not one that many people wish to follow. This is demonstrated clearly by the fact that although there are many young people needing work, few opt to take employment in a field where the wage is over twice the minimum. Can it simply be the fear of taking clothes off in public that keeps them away? The answer to this question seems to rest, even in the early part of the twenty-first century, in a widespread fear of peer group condemnation.

Many people shrink in horror at the idea of appearing nude before others and propose that situation as their worst nightmare. In fact many people who paint and draw from the nude model would not be prepared to pose themselves. There is even an unwritten and unspoken distinction between models and artists. Many students and artists seem to imagine that models are in some way inferior and many tutors seem to be similarly afflicted. In reality, of course, the co-operation of the model is a tacit essential. If a model can hold a pose which presents challenges to the students at all levels, and is not subsequently offended by the sometimes grotesque drawings done by the less observant, then the learning process will be swift.

Models who have no experience of drawing need to know that good poses are those in which the limbs and torso are arranged so that the 'frog pinned down for dissection' and 'soldier standing to attention' or 'at ease' is avoided. Feet at differing levels and one leg or arm straight – less bent than the other; a twist in the torso; and head held at an angle to the spine are ingredients of a good pose.

Where there are many drawing from around a central podium, the model for short poses should be sure to change the direction faced for each new pose so as to present back and side views to all, in turn, at the model's discretion.

OVERHEARD IN A STUDIO

Overheard by a model when the tyrant-tutor was absent – out of ear-shot:

"She is a perambulating example of the more petty the power the greater the urge to exercise it. The only way to deal with her is to say "Yes! thank you VERY much.""

FINAL WORD

As was mentioned in the Foreword, this conclusion is the final word. If any reader has managed to get thus far and has come to see that they too may join in the activities of some local life classes, to discover a new freedom of expression, then our target has been met.

Some, we hope, will even take the plunge and become part-time models, others may join in groups and classes. Both will find that, as with bungey-jumping or jumping off the high-diving board, or even solo-piloting an aeroplane, there is a wonderful sense of new freedom. Also there is a sense of fellowship with the others who have denied the fears of disapproval of others who have not discovered that the beauty of the human form reposes in its unique individuality and that none of us are perfect and all of us are filled with interesting differences between each and everyone of our kith.

There is FREEDOM in many senses in being the model, the focus of the group who are intent upon discovering from us, the models, the truth about their own concept of humanity. It is the artists' duty to transmit this illusion by means of a two or three dimensional representation of the essence of us (the models) as an improvement upon nature or a synthesis of the essence of individuality, to others.

The freedom of being as we were created in the nakedness of the holy sadhu, hermit or model of man, is to be without fear of what others might think or say. We are what we are.

That is the psychological freedom from the physiological reality.

There is also the physical freedom of knowing there is no danger in being too cold or unable to control our muscles so that we do not move.

It is the same fear that a sniper has – he who has to keep unseen will himself become a victim of the unseen.

BIBLIOGRAPHY

BORZELLO, Frances

The Artists' Model
Junction Books, 1982
ISBN 0862 4506 83

CONSTANCE, Diana

Life Class Drawing
Quarto Books, 1991
ISBN 0712 6505 20

CORSECK, Jane

Painting Figures in Light
Watson-Guptill Publishers, New York.
ISBN 0823 036316

EPSTEIN, Jacob

Jacob Epstein, an Autobiography
London, 1940

GOMBRICH E.H.

Art and Illusion
Phaidon Press 1960-86
ISBN 7148 1756 2

HARTLEY D and
ELLIOT, Margaret M

*Life and Work of the People of England in
the 18th Century*
Batsford, London, 1931

KELLY, Francis

The Studio and the Artist
David and Charles Newton Abbot,
1974

MARSH, Jan

The Legend of Elizabeth E Siddal
Quartet Books, 1989
ISBN 0704 326175

MARSH, Jan — *The Pre-Raphaelite Sisterhood*
Quartet Books, 1998
ISBN 0704 3016 95

ORMOND, Leonee & Richard — *The Biography of Lord Leighton*
The Paul Mellon Centre for Studies in British Art
ISBN 0300 0189 67.

RAPPOPORT, Angelo Soloman — *Famous Artists and their Models*
St Paul, 1919

SEGAL, Muriel
FURLONG, Iris
(co-author) — *Dolly on the Dais*
subtitled *The Artist's Model in Perspective*
Gentry Books, 1972

SMITH, Alison edited by — *Exposed, the Victorian Nude*
Tate Publishing, 2002
ISBN 185 437 372

ACRONYMS

ACUN is our abbreviation for academic undress.

Angels
Consider
Undress
Normal

Or

Artistic
Condition
Usually
Noticeable

Or

Always
Completely
Uninhibited
Nudity

Or

Agreeably
Comfortable
Unashamed
Nakedness

EUPHEMISMS

The term for the art of not calling a spade a spade is 'euphemism'.

"There was a man,
such a Prude
he could not mouth the word Nude."

(Apologies to the author of the parodied "there was a girl who was so pure she could not mouth the word manure.")

Nudity has become a focus of the attention of euphemism coiners. There are countless examples: "In the noddy, in the altogether, in the birthday-suit, as naked as the day he was born, Godiva, skinny-dipping," to quote just a few. Even among nudists, who like to be known as naturists, there is a reverse prudery and the terms clothed and unclothed are too simple, as naked is biblically associated with shame, so nudists call non-nudists 'beached textile'. Now textile is the term used for fashion design students especially in art colleges. Yet these students are usually particularly good at life drawing and because fashion models are often exceptionally long-legged they like to use models who are also very long-legged, or to put it the other way round, they do not like to draw from short, fat dumpy models.

DICTIONARY DEFINITIONS

Some dictionary definitions associated with the vagueness of Euphemisms. These may help to illuminate the parallel between words and lines in a drawing and their meaning.

Dr Samuel Johnson, the first great Lexicographer, is regarded as an authority on the meanings of words. Pictures are said to be worth a thousand words. So his views on the use of words relating to Life studios are of interest. But as he avoided mention of 'obscenities', and rebuked a lady who asked him why his Dictionary had no lewd words, with

"I do not daub my fingers – but I note you searched for obscenities," which he defined as 'lewdness, impurity of thought, naughty bad wicked…' By contrast he thought 'proper' in its 10th meaning ('tall, lusty: handsome with bulk') to be a **low** word; maybe as in Heraldic supporters. Shakespeare is quoted as having written "proper nakedness". 'Pose' had no meaning as a noun for Sam J. beyond 'heaviness or stupifaction' and 'to put to a stand or stop' (from which one might deduce that the static pose on a podium is derived).

The word **model** does not feature in the sense of a person or the human form, in the 4th edition of the 1st edition of SJ's Dictionary of English Words. So it can be inferred that there were no Life-classes in or near Fleet Street where he had his rooms in 1754. Further to that the hacks of that street-of-shame were not interested in exposing nudity. But Dr J does give for **LIFE** an (8th) meaning: '**Living** form as opposed to copies'. The 3rd example is from Colliers *of the Entertainment of Books*: 'He that would be master, <u>must draw from *life*</u> as well as the original and join theory and experience together'. Whether this means to draw with a pencil or to <u>extract from</u>, as in drawing water from a well, is unclear as is the meaning of the <u>original</u>, say, a painting being copied.

Nudity appears after **Nudation** which is defined as the 'act of make bare'. Only one example is given for each. Dryden is quoted 'There are no such licences in poetry or any more in painting to design and colour obscene *nudities*'; can we take it that there were licences for non-obscene nudes? Or is the implication that all nudes were obscene in the 1750s? Does a model at the end of a session or before a tea-break *denudate*? If so then on resumption of posing the command might be *renudate*. Or get another booking (*re a new date?*).

The word **take** had, in the 1st edition, 113 sense according to Simon Winchester in *The Surgeon from Crowthorne*: 'To perform what one does in removing clothing' (*take-off*). Amongst the 117 quotes in the Dublin 4th edition revised by SJ (which omits the foregoing) are #94: 'He [Moses] *took* the veil *off* in the temple', Exodus xxxiv:34. #92 is of interest: a quotation from Addison, '*take off* all their models in wood'. This does not mean a wood-carving life-class, but making in large scale some furniture/boat/house which had been planned in miniature model.

#8 is a quotation from the *Decay of Piety* - 'If I renounce virtue, though naked, then I do it yet more when she is thus beautified to allure the eye and *take* the heart.'

Index

Sherborne

ArtsLink

Sherborne House
Newland
Sherborne
Dorset DT9 3JG
Telephone 01935 815899

MODELS FOR LIFE DRAWING

Fee: £8.00 per hour plus travel expenses of 16p/mile

Name:

Address:

Telephone:

Class:

Venue:

Dates: Time:

Fee: hours at £8.00/hour

Travel   miles at 16p/mile x 2

TOTAL:

Signatures: For ArtsLink

_____ Model

Please sign and return in the enclosed envelope.
Payment by cheque will be at the conclusion of the contract period.

Sherborne ArtsLink Limited – Co. no. 2471382
Non profit-making educational charity Registered no. 1007680
Patrons: Sir Peter Ustinov – Gerald Pitman MBE FRSA

RE-ORDER AND FEEDBACK FORM

To Melrose Books, the Publisher of *Academic Undress*
At: Melrose Books
St Thomas' Place
Ely
Cambridgeshire
CB7 4GG

info@melrosebooks.com
info@academicundress.net

Please send me __ copies of the 2nd Edition of *Academic Undress* at £14.99 per copy.

Name: _____

Adress: _____

_____

_____

_____

Post Code: _____

Country: _____

I undertake to pay on receipt of an invoice £_____

I enclosemy suggestions for possible inclusion in the 2nd Edition.

SUGGESTIONS FOR INCLUSION IN THE 2ND EDITION OF *ACADEMIC UNDRESS*